FIND OUT WHAT'S IN THE NEW TAX LAW— WHAT IT WILL COST YOU, AND WHAT YOU MAY SAVE!

What will happen to your taxes under the new tax law? You'll find out all the answers in this up-to-the-minute guide—specially created by the tax experts at the J. K. Lasser Institute! It's packed with valuable information, explanations, and advice on all the most important points in the 1993 law, including:

*Higher personal income tax rates
*Tax increases retroactive to the start of 1993
*Cutbacks on deductions for travel and entertainment expenses
*Special natural disaster relief provisions
*Cuts in deductions for job-related expenses
*New estimated tax "safe harbor" provisions
*New tax-saving opportunities for real estate operators
*New two-tier tax computation for Social Security benefits

GET ALL THE FACTS—AND START YOUR PLANNING NOW!

J.K. LASSER'S™ WHAT THE NEW TAX LAW MEANS TO YOU

■ YOUR GUIDE TO THE MAJOR NEW TAX ACT ■ PROTECT YOUR HOME, SAVINGS, AND RETIREMENT BENEFITS

POCKET BOOKS

New York London Toronto Sydney Tokyo Singapore

An *Original* Publication of POCKET BOOKS

POCKET BOOKS, a division of Simon & Schuster Inc.
1230 Avenue of the Americas, New York, NY 10020

ISBN: 0-671-88566-9

First Pocket Books printing November 1993

10 9 8 7 6 5 4 3 2 1

POCKET and colophon are registered trademarks of Simon & Schuster Inc.

Printed in the U.S.A.

CONTENTS

PREFACE

The 1993 tax law differs from other recently passed tax laws in that it has not been pitched to the public as a tax-reform measure. Instead, it has an unconcealed and blunt purpose: to raise tax revenues. The tax increases it includes are selective in thrust because of political maneuvering, and political posturing almost led to its defeat in Congress—its passage turning on a single vote. However, a new law has the same effect whether passed by a hundred votes or one, so you should be aware of how this new law affects your tax liability.

If you drive a car, you will pay increased fuel taxes. If you earn substantial income, your tax liability may be higher this year because of the retroactive effect of the new higher brackets. If you are retired and receiving Social Security benefits, you may also be subject to higher taxes next year. Besides these increases, the new law also reduces or eliminates certain business and job-related expense deductions. In other areas, however, there are new tax-saving opportunities such as the elimination of the passive rental loss rules for real estate operators. Some rules take effect retroactively in 1993; others, not until 1994.

You'll find an overview of all these changes in the special table titled "Highlights of the New Tax Law" at the beginning of this book. Subsequent chapters explain each provision in detail and offer tax-planning suggestions. We hope that the information in these pages will help you protect your money and plan wisely now that the new law has been passed.

The J. K. Lasser editors

J.K. LASSER'S™ WHAT THE NEW TAX LAW MEANS TO YOU

1

HIGHLIGHTS OF THE NEW TAX LAW

Tax Item	Prior Law	New Law
Personal Tax rates	Three tax brackets: 15%, 28%, 31% and a 28% ceiling on net long-term capital gain.	Four tax brackets: 15%, 28%, 31%, and 36%. 10% surtax will be imposed on taxable income over $250,000. Capital gain tax ceiling of 28% is unaffected. The surtax built into the rates makes the 36% bracket actually 39.6%. The rates are retroactive to the beginning of 1993. However, an increased tax attributable to the rate increase may be paid over a three-year period.
Phaseout of personal exemptions	Personal exemptions were reduced or eliminated when adjusted gross income exceeded certain amounts.	Phaseout is made a permanent part of the law.
Reduction of itemized deductions	Certain itemized deductions were reduced if adjusted gross income exceeded certain amounts.	Phaseout is made a permanent part of the law.
Alternative Minimum Tax	Rate was 24% on AMT taxable income. AMT exemption was	Two rates starting in 1993: 26% on AMT taxable incomes up to

	allowed for married filing jointly with taxable income of up to $40,000, single persons or heads of households with taxable income of up to $30,000, and married filing separately with taxable income of up to $20,000.	$175,000 and 28% on excess. AMT exemption amounts are increased to $45,000 for married filing jointly, to $33,750 for single persons and heads of households, and to $22,500 for married filing separately. The increase is effective in 1993, but tax attributable to the increase is not payable over a three-year period.
Charitable donations of appreciated property	For purposes of the alternative minimum tax (AMT), a taxpayer could not deduct the full value of long-term capital gain property contributed after June 30, 1992. The taxpayer's deduction was effectively limited to the basis of the contributed property.	The AMT preference rule for all donations of appreciated property is repealed. This rule applies to charitable contributions of tangible personal property made after June 30, 1992, and to other types of appreciated property contributed after 1992.
Estimated tax "safe harbor" rules	Taxpayers in certain income ranges were not able to avoid penalty by paying 100% of the prior year's tax.	Starting in 1994, the 100% payment rule may be used if the prior year's adjusted gross income is $150,000 or less ($75,000 or less if married filing separately). A 110%

Tax Item	Prior Law	New Law
		payment rule applies for adjusted gross incomes exceeding $150,000 ($75,000 if married filing separately).
Social Security benefits	Social Security benefits could be tax-free if adjusted gross income was below the base amount of $25,000 for single persons or $32,000 for married persons filing a joint return. Married persons filing separately who lived together at any time during the year were not allowed any base amount. When benefits exceeded the base amount, up to 50% of benefits could be taxable.	Starting in 1994, the percentage of Social Security benefits subject to tax increases from 50% to 85% for persons with incomes over $34,000 if single and $44,000 if married filing jointly.
Withholding tax on bonuses	20% withholding tax rate.	28% withholding tax rate on all bonuses, commissions, and other supplemental payments made after 1993.

Earned income credit	The earned income credit was composed of a basic credit, a supplemental credit for workers with a child under the age of one, and a supplemental credit for certain health insurance premium expenses. In 1993 the maximum EIC for one child was $1,434, and for two or more children, $1,511. The maximum supplemental credit in 1993 was $388, and the maximum supplemental health insurance credit was $465. All three credit components were subject to a phaseout rule.	Starting in 1994, the basic credit for families with children increases to $2,038 for one child, to $2,500 for two or more children. The supplemental newborn child and health insurance credit is repealed. For the first time, the credit is made available to childless workers (between the ages of 26 and 64).
Wage ceiling for Medicare tax	Payroll and self-employment tax funding Medicare is 1.45% applied to a base of up to $135,000.	The base ceiling of $135,000 is removed for figuring the 1.45% tax starting in 1994.
Tax-free employer-paid education	After June 30, 1992, employees were taxed on educational assistance provided under a qualifying employer-financed educational	Tuition assistance under a qualified employer-financed educational plan is tax-free up to $5,250 as of July 1, 1992. Refunds for bene-

Tax Item	Prior Law	New Law
	assistance program. Before July 1, 1992, such assistance was tax-free up to $5,250.	fits received after that date may be obtained through the employer.
Disaster tax relief	No similar provision.	Residents in an area designated a disaster zone after September 30, 1991, may avoid tax on insurance reimbursements for certain personal property losses. If a home was destroyed, the homeowner can buy a replacement home and defer tax on any gain within a four-year period.
Moving expenses to new job location	Qualifying unreimbursed moving expenses to a new job location were deductible only if you claimed itemized deductions. A 35-mile distance test was enforced. Only certain types of expenses were fully deductible, such as the cost of moving household goods and the travel costs of the	Starting in 1994, you may deduct moving expenses whether or not you claim itemized deductions. However, the distance test is increased to at least 50 miles. Only expenses of moving household goods and traveling to new locations are deductible. No deduction will be allowed for temporary liv-

	taxpayer and family members. Other expenses, such as the costs of pre-move house-hunting trips or temporary quarters at the new job location, were deductible within limits.	ing costs, pre-move trips to look for quarters, and costs of buying and selling a residence.
Club dues	If certain tests were met, dues paid to country, social and athletic clubs were deductible.	No deduction of such costs is allowed after 1993.
Travel costs of spouse on business trips	Under limited circumstances, the travel cost of a spouse accompanying a business person on a business trip could be deductible.	After 1993, no deduction will be allowed for costs allocated to spouses unless they are employees traveling for business.
Proof of cash donations	Cancelled checks were accepted as proof of all cash donations.	For separate donations of $250 or more made after 1993, a receipt from the charity is needed to support the deduction.
Deduction of self-employed health insurance costs	Self-employed were not allowed to deduct any part of health insurance costs paid after June 30, 1992.	The deduction is reinstated as of July 1, 1992. The deduction also may be claimed in 1993. An amended return may be filed to claim the deduction in 1992 for

Tax Item	Prior Law	New Law
		premiums paid in 1992 after June 30, 1992.
Meal and entertainment costs	80% of the cost of business meals and entertainment were deductible.	Only 50% of such costs are deductible after 1993.
Estate and gift taxes	Top estate and gift tax rate of 50% was in effect for taxable transfers of over $2.5 million made after 1992.	Reintroduces top tax rates of 53% and 55% on taxable transfers exceeding $2.5 million. Prior law phaseout range is also reinstated.
Capital gain exclusion for small business investments	No such provision.	To encourage investments in small businesses, a 50% exclusion for capital gains applies to stocks bought after August 10, 1993, and held at least five years in certain small business corporations.
Empowerment and enterprise zones	No such provision.	Nine empowerment zones and 95 enterprise communities to be organized in 1994 and 1995. In empowerment zones, qualified businesses may claim a 20% credit

		for wages paid to workers living in that zone and an additional first-year expense allowance of $20,000. Businesses in enterprise zones are only entitled to special financing.
Professional real estate operators	Rental losses were generally deductible only against passive income. However, if you managed rental real estate with adjusted gross income of $100,000 or less, you could deduct up to $25,000 of your rental loss. The disallowed losses could be carried over to later years, subject to the same restrictions.	You may avoid passive loss treatment of rental losses if you are an active real estate operator in a development, construction, rental management, leasing, or brokerage business. Activity tests require more than 50% activity and at least 750 hours during a taxable year. The new rules are effective after 1993.
Depreciation recovery period for commercial realty	The recovery period for buildings placed in service after December 31, 1986, was 27.5 years for residential rental property and 31.5 years for nonresidential real property. The method of recovery was	A recovery period of 39 years applies to nonresidential property placed in service after May 12, 1993.

Tax Item	Prior Law	New Law
	the straight-line method using a mid-month convention.	
First-year expensing	Instead of claiming depreciation, you could deduct up to $10,000 of the cost of business equipment placed in service in a taxable year.	The $10,000 ceiling is increased to $17,500 for property placed in service in taxable years beginning after December 31, 1992.
Low-income housing credit	Up until June 30, 1992, a low-income housing tax credit was allowed in annual installments over ten years for newly constructed to substantially rehabilitated low-income rental housing.	The credit is made permanent as of June 30, 1992.
Corporate tax rates	There were three corporate tax rates: 15% of the first $50,000 of taxable income, 25% on taxable income between $50,000 and $75,000, and the top rate of 34% for taxable income that exceeded $75,000. For corporations with	A maximum 35% tax rate applies to corporations with taxable incomes in excess of $10 million. Corporations with taxable incomes in excess of $15 million also have to recapture the benefit of the 34% rate by increasing their

	taxable income in excess of $100,000, the benefit of the 15% and 25% brackets was phased out under a recapture rule.	tax liability by 3% for income in excess of $15 million. The tax increase here may not exceed $100,000. The new rates apply retroactively to taxable years starting on or after January 1, 1993. Fiscal years starting in 1992 and ending in 1993 are subject to the new rates on an allocated basis.
Estimated tax for corporations	Generally, corporations were required to make four timely estimated tax payments to the IRS to avoid a penalty, based on 97% of the corporation's projected current-year tax liability, or 97% of projected liability under an annualized income method. The general 97% requirement was scheduled to continue through the 1996 tax year and then drop to 91% requirement.	For tax years starting after 1993, a corporation must base quarterly payments on 100% of current tax liability, unless it qualifies to pay the estimate based on the prior year's tax.

Tax Item	Prior Law	New Law
Research and experimentation credit	Before June 30, 1992, a 20% tax credit was applied to incremental research expenses.	The credit is extended permanently, applying to 20% of the qualifying research expenses in excess of a historic base amount. In addition, special credit computation rules apply to start-up companies.
Targeted jobs credit	Until it expired on June 30, 1992, the targeted jobs credit gave a tax credit to employers who hired individuals in nine designated categories.	The credit is extended through 1994 and retroactively to June 30, 1992.
Cap on high-earner retirement contributions	Retirement plan contributions and benefits for higher-paid executives and owner-employees were limited by annual compensation limit of $235,840.	The annual compensation limit is cut back to $150,000 for plan years starting after 1993.
Deduction of executive pay	Under the law, there was no cap on the deductible pay of highly paid executives.	For tax years after 1993, deductions of executive pay exceeding $1 million are generally not al-

		lowed, unless the pay is linked to the executive's productivity.
Security dealer's inventory	Could be valued at cost or market, whichever was lower.	Must use fair market value at year end. Effective for tax years ending on or after December 31, 1993.
Lobbying expenses	They were generally deductible.	No deduction is allowed for costs incurred after 1993.
Qualified home mortgages	Up until June 30, 1992, mortgage credit certificates were available to finance the purchase of a principal residence or to borrow funds for certain home improvements. Generally, a qualifying principal residence could not cost more than 90% of the average area purchase price; 110% in certain targeted areas. The law allowed a tax credit for interest paid on the mortgage. The maximum annual credit was $2,000. Interest paid but not qualifying for the credit was deductible as home mortgage interest.	Authority to issue qualified home mortgage credit certificates is renewed as of July 1, 1992.

Tax Item	Prior Law	New Law
Tax credit for FICA taxes paid on tips	No provision.	Restaurants and other food or beverage establishments may claim a tax credit that partially offsets FICA taxes (Social Security and Medicare) paid after 1993 on tips reported by employees. The credit is limited to FICA taxes on tips that exceed the minimum wage.

2
PERSONAL TAX RATE INCREASES

OVERVIEW

First and foremost, the new tax law increases personal tax rates. However, many taxpayers are not affected by the new income tax rates of 36% and 39.6%. Those untouched are single filers with taxable income of up to $115,000; heads of households with taxable income of up to $127,500; married couples filing jointly with taxable income up to $140,000; and married couples filing separately with taxable income of up to $70,000. However, starting in 1994, Social Security recipients with far lower incomes will pay more tax on Social Security benefits subject to the new 85% exclusion rule. Payroll taxes will also increase after 1993 for high-salary earners because there will no longer be a wage base ceiling for Medicare tax purposes.

NEW TAX RATES

The new law establishes four tax bracket rates of 15%, 28%, 31%, and 36%. In addition, a 10% surtax is imposed on taxable income over $250,000 ($125,000 if married filing separately). The surtax does not apply to capital gains. The surtax has the effect of creating a 39.6% top bracket. These increases take effect retroactively as of January 1, 1993. Because of the phaseout of personal exemptions and the 3% reduction of itemized deductions, the actual top effective rate may be 42% or more, depending on the number of exemptions claimed.

On the following pages, you will find new tax rate schedules. You may use these to estimate your 1993 taxes. When you prepare your 1993 tax return and your taxable income is less than $100,000, you will use official tax tables to find your tax. When you use those tables, you do not compute your tax mathematically; you first figure your taxable income, then turn to your income bracket and look for the tax liability listed in the column for your filing status. You will find the tables in our annual tax guide, *J.K. Lasser's Your Income Tax.*

Single Taxpayer:

If taxable income is: *The tax is:*

Over—	*But not over—*		*Of the amount over—*
$ 0	$ 22,100	15%	$ 0
22,100	53,500	$ 3,315 + 28%	22,100
53,500	115,000	12,107 + 31%	53,500
115,000	250,000	31,172 + 36%	115,000
250,000		79,772 + 39.6%	250,000

Married Persons Filing Jointly:

If taxable income is: *The tax is:*

Over—	*But not over—*		*Of the amount over—*
$ 0	$ 36,900	15%	$ 0
36,900	89,150	$ 5,535.00 + 28%	36,900
89,150	140,000	20,165.00 + 31%	89,150
140,000	250,000	35,928.50 + 36%	140,000
250,000		75,528.50 + 39.6%	250,000

Head of Household:

If taxable income is: *The tax is:*

Over—	*But not over—*		*Of the amount over—*
$ 0	$ 29,600	15%	$ 0
29,600	76,400	$ 4,440 + 28%	29,600
76,400	127,500	17,544 + 31%	76,400
127,500	250,000	33,385 + 36%	127,500
250,000		77,485 + 39.6%	250,000

Married Persons Filing Separately:

If taxable income is: *The tax is:*

Over—	*But not over—*		*Of the amount over—*
$ 0	$ 18,450	15%	$ 0
18,450	44,575	$ 2,767.50 + 28%	18,450
44,575	70,000	10,082.50 + 31%	44,575
70,000	125,000	17,964.25 + 36%	70,000
125,000		37,764.25 + 39.6%	125,000

Here are some examples illustrating how to use these tax rate schedules.

Examples

1. You file as a head of household with taxable income of $103,000.

Tax on first $ 76,400	$17,544.00
31% tax on excess $26,600	$ 8,246.00
Total tax	$25,790.00

2. You are married and file a joint return with taxable income of $130,000.

Tax on first $89,150	$ 20,165.00
31% tax on excess $40,850	$12,663.50
Total tax	$32,828.50

10% SURTAX FOR SUBSTANTIAL INCOME EARNERS

The new law places a 10% surtax on taxable income over $250,000 earned by single persons, heads of households, and married persons filing jointly. For married persons filing separately, the threshold amount is $125,000.

The surtax is built into the tax rate schedules by applying a 39.6% rate to non-capital-gain taxable income in excess of the $250,000 ($125,000 for married filing separately) threshold.

Example

The Smiths use a joint return to report adjusted gross income of $510,000, with itemized deductions of $40,000 which are reduced to $27,953 by the 3% reduction of itemized deductions. Their personal exemptions are completely eliminated by the 2% phaseout. As a result of the 36% bracket and the 10% surtax, the Smiths now pay $25,457 more in taxes than they would have paid under the prior law tax rates. The couple's 1993 tax under the new rates is calculated as follows, with a calculation under the old rates for comparison.

Adjusted gross income	$510,000
Less itemized deductions	$ 27,953
Taxable income	$482,047

Total tax under prior law tax rates. Using the prior rates for married couples filing jointly, the Smiths' tax would have been $141,963.

Tax on the first $89,150	$ 20,165
Tax on the excess $392,897 ($482,047–$89,150 at 31% rate)	$121,798
Total tax	$141,963

Total tax under new law rates. Under the new 36% bracket and the effective 39.6% bracket created by the surtax, the Smiths' 1993 tax is raised substantially, to $167,420—$25,457 more than it would have been under the old rates.

Tax on the first $250,000 (36% bracket starts at $140,000)	$ 75,529
Tax on the excess $232,047 ($482,047–$250,000 at surtax rate of 39.6%)	$ 91,891
Total tax	$167,420

MARRIED COUPLES PENALIZED

The new tax law has the effect of creating a so-called "marriage penalty": a two-income married couple filing jointly pays more tax than two single persons living together with the same total income. The new 36% tax bracket for married couples filing jointly applies to taxable incomes of over $140,000; for single persons, over $115,000. Thus, two unmarried people, each with a taxable income of $110,000 (× 2 = $220,000), are subject to a top bracket of 31% while a married couple filing jointly with the same combined $220,000 of income pay a 36% tax on the excess over $140,000.

And there's more. Consider as well the new surtax on taxable income of $250,000 or more. Married couples are not allowed a higher base amount on joint returns. Whether you are single or married filing jointly does not matter. Once you top the $250,000 base amount, the surtax applies equally. Thus if single persons with separate taxable incomes of $150,000 marry and file jointly, they will pay a surtax on $50,000 based on their combined $300,000 income. If they remained single, they would not be subject to the surtax. Furthermore, as single taxpayers, they could each have taxable incomes of $250,000 for a combined total of $500,000 without being subject to the surtax.

TAX PAYMENT DEFERRAL FOR 1993 TAX INCREASE

If you are subject to the new 36% and 39.6% brackets, you may not immediately have to pay the entire tax increase. You may elect to pay the extra tax in three equal annual installments, the first being due on April 15, 1994 (even if a 1993 filing extension is obtained). Interest will not be charged on the deferred payments.

The installment election applies only to the extra tax due as a result of the top rate being increased from 31% to 36% or 39.6%. It does not apply to higher alternative minimum taxes (AMT).

ESTIMATED TAX PENALTY RELIEF FOR 1993 TAX INCREASE

If you earn substantial income that places you in the new higher tax brackets, you may want to increase your final estimated tax payment due January 18, 1994. However, if you do not amend your estimated tax, you will not be subject to an estimated tax penalty to the extent that your underpayment is attributed to the tax rate increase.

NEW ESTIMATED "SAFE HARBOR" TEST FOR SUBSTANTIAL INCOME EARNERS

Until the new law comes into effect in 1994, higher-income taxpayers may be barred from basing estimated tax payments on 100% of a prior year's tax. If you paid estimated tax installments in 1990, 1991, or 1992, or were charged an underpayment penalty in any of those years, and your income exceeded certain limits, you may not use the 100% prior-year exception to avoid a 1993 penalty if you underestimate your tax. This restriction applies if your 1993 adjusted gross income exceeds $75,000 ($37,500 if married filing separately) and if, after certain adjustments, your 1993 adjusted gross income also exceeds your 1992 adjusted gross income by more than $40,000 ($20,000 if married filing separately).

New tax law. The restriction just described is repealed starting in 1994. If you file a 1993 return that covers 12 months, you may avoid the penalty by figuring and paying as your 1994 estimated tax an amount based on a percentage of your 1993 tax. If your 1993 adjusted gross income (AGI) is $150,000 or less ($75,000 or less if married filing separately), you may avoid a 1994 penalty by making estimated payments of at least 100% of your 1993 tax. If your 1993 AGI exceeds $150,000 ($75,000 if married filing separately), you may avoid a penalty if the 1994 payments are 110% of the 1993 tax. If neither the 100% nor 110% "safe harbor" is used, estimated tax payments have to equal at least 90% of the 1994 tax liability to avoid a penalty.

CAPITAL GAINS TAX CEILING

Capital gain or loss treatment applies to sales of property held for investment or personal purposes, except for certain items excluded by law from the category of capital assets. Sales of capital assets are reported on Schedule D of Form 1040. On Schedule D, long-term capital gain or loss applies to sales of assets held for more than a year, and short-term capital gain or loss to sales of assets held for one year or less.

Net capital gains are added to your other income and subject to regular tax rates if your top rate is 15% or 28%. However, if your top tax rate exceeds 28%, long-term gains in excess of short-term losses are subject to a top rate of 28%.

Under the new law, the 28% tax ceiling for net long-term capital gains remains unchanged. If your tax bracket exceeds 28%, you use the following alternative method to apply the 28% ceiling rate:

1. Enter your taxable income. $______
2. Enter your net capital gain (net long-term capital gain less net short-term capital loss). ______
3. Subtract line 2 from line 1. This is taxable income without net capital gain. ______
4. Enter $22,100 if you use single rates*
   $36,900 if you use joint rates*
   $29,600 if you use head of household rates*
   $18,450 if you use married filing separately rates* ______
5. Enter the greater of line 3 or line 4. ______
6. Subtract line 5 from line 1. This is the amount of capital gain that benefits from the 28% rate. ______
7. Figure the amount of tax on line 5 from the tax rate schedule if line 5 is $100,000 or more; use the tax tables if less than $100,000. ______
8. Multiply line 6 by 28% and enter the result. ______
9. Add lines 7 and 8. This is your total tax. $______

*These amounts are the taxable income levels above which the 28% rate starts in 1993 rate schedules.

Examples

1. The Browns file a 1993 joint return showing a taxable income of $112,000 including a net capital gain of $5,000. Taxable income of $112,000 puts them in the 31% bracket. Their tax is $27,099.

1. Taxable income	$112,000
2. Net capital gain	5,000
3. Taxable income without net capital gain	107,000
4. Starting point for 28% tax rate on joint return	36,900
5. Greater of line 3 or 4	107,000
6. Line 1 minus line 5. This is net capital gain subject to ceiling	5,000
7. Tax on line 5 before adding capital gain tax	25,699
8. 28% of $5,000 on line 6	1,400
9. Add lines 7 and 8. This is the alternative tax including the 28% ceiling for net capital gain	$27,099

2. The Smiths file a 1993 joint return showing a taxable income of $180,000 including a net capital gain of $5,000. Taxable gain of $150,000 places them in the 36% bracket. Their tax is $49,929.

1. Taxable income	$180,000
2. Net capital gain	5,000
3. Taxable income without net capital gain	175,000
4. Starting point for 28% tax rate on joint return	36,900
5. Greater of line 3 or 4	175,000
6. Line 1 minus line 5. This is net capital gain subject to ceiling	5,000
7. Tax on line 5 before adding capital gain tax	48,529
8. 28% of $5,000 on line 6	1,400
9. Add lines 7 and 8. This is the alternative tax including the 28% ceiling for net capital gain	$49,929

MEDICARE WAGE CEILING REMOVED

FICA (Federal Insurance Contributions Act) withholdings are employee contributions for Social Security and Medicare hospital insurance coverage. Employers must match employee withholdings. The amount withheld is figured on wages and is not affected by marital status, number of exemptions, or the fact that the employee may be over age 65 and is collecting Social Security.

FICA tax is imposed on the following: regular salary, commissions, bonuses, vacation pay, the first six months of sick pay, Christmas bonuses, cash tips, lump-sum settlements of wage disputes, and contributions to cash or deferred (401(k)) pay plans or salary-reduction contributions to a simplified employee pension (SEP) or tax-sheltered annuity plans. It also applies to group-term insurance coverage over $50,000.

FICA tax is not imposed on the following: the value of tax-free meals and lodgings and reimbursements for substantiated travel or entertainment expenses or for job-related moving expenses.

FICA tax is imposed on employees and employers up to a maximum amount of employee wages.

The FICA rate is 7.65% of which 6.20% is for Social Security, retirement and disability benefits and 1.45% is for Medicare hospital insurance. For wages paid to covered employees in 1993, the 6.20% rate will apply to a wage base of up to $57,600. The 1.45% Medicare rate will apply to employee wages of up to $135,000.

Self-employed individuals are subject to tax on net earnings, equivalent to the employer and employee shares of FICA tax, which provides funds for Social Security and Medicare benefits. Self-employment tax must be paid even if a self-employed person is over age 65 and receives Social Security benefits.

The self-employment tax rate is made up of two rates: a 15.3% rate which applies in 1993 to a taxable earnings base of up to $57,600, and a 2.9% rate on a taxable earnings base exceeding $57,600 up to $135,000.

The Medicare tax ceiling on both wages and self-employment income is increased annually for inflation, as is the Social Security component of the tax.

New tax law. The $135,000 cap (as adjusted annually) on wages and self-employment earnings subject to the Medicare tax is eliminated. After 1993, *all* wages and earnings are subject to the Medicare tax.

It is estimated that 1.2 million high-wage workers will be affected by the increase.

ITEMIZED DEDUCTION LIMITATION EXTENDED

Individuals get a greater tax savings by claiming itemized deductions that exceed the standard deduction for their filing status. Itemized deductions include unreimbursed medical and dental expenses, casualty and theft losses, charitable contributions, qualified home mortgage interest, investment interest, state and local income and property taxes, unreimbursed employee business expenses, investment and tax preparation expenses, certain moving expenses, and gambling losses (to the extent that they do not exceed winnings). Various floors apply to medical expenses, casualty deductions, job expenses and other miscellaneous expenses.

If your 1993 adjusted gross income (AGI) exceeds $108,450 ($54,225 if married filing separately), allowable itemized deductions *other than* gambling losses, medical expenses, casualty and theft losses, and investment interest expenses are reduced by 3% of the AGI over $108,450 (or $54,225). Otherwise allowable deductions, however, may not be reduced by more than 80%. The $108,450 and $54,225 amounts are subject to annual inflation adjustments. Under prior law, the phaseout was to apply for taxable years before 1996. For 1996 and later years the full deduction was to be allowed.

New tax law. The 3% reduction of itemized deductions is now a permanent feature of the tax law. The current $108,450 (or $54,225) threshold will be increased annually for inflation.

PHASEOUT OF PERSONAL EXEMPTIONS EXTENDED

In determining taxable income, an individual taxpayer is entitled to a deduction for each allowable personal exemption. A separate exemption is allowed for the taxpayer, the taxpayer's spouse, and each dependent of the taxpayer. For 1993, the deduction allowable for each exemption is $2,350. This amount is increased annually for inflation.

Taxpayers whose adjusted gross income (AGI) exceeds a threshold amount must reduce or eliminate the deduction for personal exemptions. For 1993, the thresholds are $162,700 for married filing jointly, $135,600 for heads of households, $108,450 for single persons, and $81,350 for married filing separately. The threshold amounts will be increased annually for inflation.

A taxpayer generally must reduce each personal exemption by 2% for every $2,500 of AGI above the applicable threshold. For married persons filing separately, the 2% phaseout applies to every $1,250 of AGI or part of $1,250 above the applicable threshold.

Under prior law, the phaseout of personal exemption deductions was to last only until 1996.

New tax law. The 2% phaseout of personal exemptions is now permanent.

TAX COST OF EXCEEDING THE THRESHOLDS FOR THE EXEMPTION PHASEOUT AND ITEMIZED DEDUCTION REDUCTION

In figuring the tax cost of earning additional income, consider the phaseout of personal exemptions or the 3% reduction to itemized deductions. When extra income, such as from a bonus, a free-lance assignment, or a year-end sale of stock, pushes you over the *threshold* for the exemption phaseout or the 3% reduction, or if you are already over the threshold, the marginal tax rate on the extra income will be higher than the stated maximum rate for ordinary income (31%, 36%, or 39.6%), or 28% for net capital gains. By earning over a threshold amount, your taxable income is increased not only by the earnings over the threshold but also by the amounts disallowed by the phaseout or the 3% reduction.

For the 3% itemized deduction reduction on 1993 returns, the adjusted gross income (AGI) threshold is $108,450, except for married persons filing separately, who are subject to a $54,225 threshold.

For the exemption phaseout, the AGI threshold is $108,450 for single persons, $135,000 for heads of household, $162,700 for married persons filing jointly and qualifying widow(er)s, and $81,350 for married persons filing separately.

Effective rate increase. The amount of the increase in the effective rate due to the exemption phaseout or 3% itemized deduction reduction can be estimated by this equation:

$$\text{Increase in effective rate} = \frac{\text{Top bracket* } \times \text{ Disallowed amount}}{\text{Excess income over threshold}}$$

*Your top bracket. For example, if you are in the 36% bracket, take 36% of the disallowed amount.

Example

You are single with salary and taxable dividends of $98,450. You claim three personal exemptions. You have itemized deductions totaling $20,000 for taxes, interest, and charitable contributions that are subject to the 3% reduction. At the end of 1993, you make a year-end sale of securities that gives you a

$44,000 net long-term capital gain, increasing your adjusted gross income (AGI) to $142,450.

By earning $34,000 over the $108,450 threshold for the 3% reduction of itemized deductions and also over the $108,450 threshold (for single persons) for the exemption phaseout, your taxable income is increased not just by $34,000 but also by the amount of the deductions that are disallowed.

Under the 3% reduction, your taxable income is increased by the $1,020 of itemized deductions that are disallowed under the 3% computation ($1,020 = 3% of the excess of your $142,450 AGI over the $108,450 threshold).

Under the phaseout rule for personal exemptions, each personal exemption claimed is reduced by 28%, from $2,350 to $1,692. The phaseout reduces your deductible exemptions from $7,050 (3 × $2,350) to $5,076 (3 × $1,692). As a result, your taxable income is increased by the $1,974 of disallowed exemptions.

Thus, the $34,000 capital gain over the $108,450 threshold increases your taxable income by $36,994: the $34,000 gain plus $2,994 (the $1,020 of disallowed itemized deductions and the $1,974 of phased-out personal exemptions).

The $34,000 gain over the threshold will be subject to the top rate of 28% net capital gain, but the $2,994 of additional taxable income due to the disallowed deductions will be taxed at 36%. As a result, the effective rate on the $34,000 gain is increased by approximately 3.17%, from 28% to 31.17%. The 3.17% increase is figured this way:

$$\frac{36\% \times \$2,994}{34,000} = 3.17\%$$

Of the extra 3.17% tax, 1.08% is attributable to the reduction of itemized deductions and 2.09% is attributable to the phaseout of personal exemptions, which is about 0.70% per exemption.

Effective tax increases due to exemption phaseout

The phaseout of exemptions is costly to taxpayers who claim several exemptions. The following chart shows the approximate effective tax increases for phased-out exemptions. The percentages are based on the income range of the example above. Percentages will vary for other income ranges.

Phaseout is-

Exemptions phased out—	*Effective rate—*
1	0.70%
2	1.40
3	2.10
4	2.80
5	3.50
6	4.20
7	4.90
8	5.60
9	6.30
10	7.00

ALTERNATIVE MINIMUM TAX INCREASED

The alternative minimum tax (AMT) is designed to recoup tax benefits that reduce or eliminate your regular income tax. AMT is triggered if it exceeds your regular income tax or you have no tax liability after claiming certain tax deductions or credits. You may incur an AMT if you have deductions for accelerated depreciation or tax shelter losses. Even when you do not have preference items, you may incur AMT if you have substantial itemized deductions that are not deductible for AMT purposes such as state and local income taxes, certain interest expenses, and miscellaneous deductions.

Taxpayers owe the higher of their regular tax or the AMT. Under prior law, they paid a flat 24% on AMT taxable income, less an exemption.

Under prior law, an AMT exemption of $40,000 was allowed for married persons filing jointly; single persons or heads of households had a $30,000 exemption; and married persons filing separately had a $20,000 exemption. However, these exemptions were phased out if AMT income exceeded specified levels that varied by filing status.

New tax law. For 1993 returns, there are two AMT rates: 26% on AMT income (after the exemption) of up to $175,000, and 28% on AMT income over $175,000.

The AMT exemption is increased to $45,000 (from $40,000) for married persons filing jointly, to $33,750 (from $30,000) for single persons and heads of households, and to $22,500 (from $20,000) for married persons filing separately.

There is no tax deferral for paying an increase attributable to the increase in AMT tax rates.

ALTERNATIVE MINIMUM TAX RELIEF FOR CHARITABLE DONATIONS OF APPRECIATED PROPERTY

In calculating taxable income for regular income tax purposes, a taxpayer is generally allowed to deduct the fair market value of property contributed to charitable organizations. However, for purposes of the alternative minimum tax (AMT), under prior law a taxpayer could not deduct the full value of long-term capital gain property contributed after June 30, 1992. Instead, the taxpayer had to treat as a tax preference, and thus add back to alternative minimum taxable income (AMTI), the amount by which the fair market value of the property exceeded the taxpayer's basis in the property.

Therefore, for AMT purposes, the taxpayer's deduction was effectively limited to the basis of the contributed property.

For donations made before July 1, 1992, an exception to this AMT rule applied for donations of tangible personal property, such as paintings or manuscripts, that had been held long term and used by the charitable donee to further its tax-exempt purpose. As a result of this exception, the appreciation on the donated property that was deductible for regular tax purposes was not treated as an AMT preference item.

New tax law. For contributions after 1992, the appreciation on donated long-term property is no longer considered a tax preference item. The new law also provides a refund opportunity to individuals who were subject to AMT in 1992 and who made charitable contributions of long-term tangible personal property in the last six months of 1992. On an amended 1992 return, the AMT preference inclusion for such property can be eliminated.

Repeal of the preference item rule benefits donors of appreciated property held long term (more than one year), such as real estate or securities, for which a deduction of fair market value is allowed for regular tax purposes. For donations of art, manuscripts or similar tangible personal property, the property must be used by the charity for uses related to its tax-exempt purposes and held long term in order for the fair market value of the property to be deductible.

For capital gain property held short term (one year or less), inventory or other ordinary income property, the charitable deduction for regular tax and AMT purposes is limited to the donor's cost.

EARNED INCOME CREDIT EXPANDED

Until now, the earned income credit (EIC) has been available only to lower-income workers who support children. The credit is refundable, meaning that if the allowable credit exceeds the individual's tax liability, the IRS will provide the taxpayer with a refund check for the difference. The new law increases the credit and greatly expands its availability.

For 1993, the earned income credit is composed of three components: (1) a basic credit adjusted for family size, (2) a supplemental credit for workers with a child under the age of one, and (3) a supplemental credit for certain health insurance premium expenses.

For 1993, the basic EIC rate is 18.5% of the first $7,750 of earned income for a worker with one child, thereby providing a maximum credit of $1,434. For a worker with two or more children, the basic credit rate is 19.5% of the first $7,750 of earned income, thereby providing a maximum credit of $1,511. The maximum supplemental credit for a child under age one in 1993 is 5% of $7,750, or $388, and the maximum supplemental health insurance credit is 6% of $7,750 or $465. All three credit components are subject to a phaseout rule. When 1993 adjusted gross income (or if greater, earned income) exceeds $12,200, the credits are gradually reduced. Under the phaseout rule, none of the credits are available if 1993 income is $23,050 or more.

New tax law. For years after 1993, the basic credit will be increased. In 1994 the maximum credit for a worker with one child will be $2,038; $2,527 for two or more children. However, the supplemental credits for health insurance covering a child, and for children under age one, will no longer be allowed. The basic credit will start to phase out where earned income exceeds $11,000.

For the first time, childless workers will be allowed a credit, but only if they are over age 25 and below age 65, have income of less than $9,000, and are not a dependent of another taxpayer.

TAX-FREE TREATMENT FOR EMPLOYER-PAID EDUCATION EXTENDED

Under a law that expired on June 30, 1992, employees were not taxed on up to $5,250 of educational assistance provided under a qualifying employer-financed educational assistance program. Such programs were subject to nondiscrimination tests to ensure that the assistance was not geared primarily to higher-paid employees. The $5,250 exclusion provided tax-free treatment for undergraduate or graduate school costs such as tuition, other fees, books, and supplies. Courses did not have to be job-related to qualify for the $5,250 exclusion unless they were for sports or hobbies unrelated to a degree program.

For job-related courses, tax-free treatment is allowed under a different statute, regardless of the value of the courses, provided the courses do not satisfy the employer's minimum education standards and do not qualify the employee for a new profession.

New tax law. The new law extends the $5,250 exclusion from July 1, 1992, to December 31, 1994. Congress requested the IRS to specify a procedure for refund claims based on courses taken in 1992 after June 30, 1992. At the time of this writing, no such procedure had yet been specified.

CREDIT BENEFITS OF QUALIFIED HOME MORTGAGE CERTIFICATES RENEWED

Under special state and local programs, up until June 1992, you could obtain "mortgage credit certificates" to finance the purchase of a principal residence or to borrow funds for certain home improvements. Generally, a qualifying principal residence could not cost more than 90% of the average area purchase price; 110% in certain targeted areas. The law allowed a tax credit for interest paid on the mortgage. The credit was computed on Form 8396 and claimed on line 44 of Form 1040. The credit equaled the interest paid multiplied by the certificate rate set by the governmental authority, up to an annual maximum of $2,000. Interest not qualifying for the credit was deductible as home mortgage interest. If you bought a home using a qualifying mortgage certificate and sold that home within nine years, you had to recapture part of the tax credit on Form 8828.

New tax law. The authority to issue qualified home mortgages is reinstated as of July 1, 1992.

The new law also extends coverage to certain two-family homes. Two-family housing may qualify if (1) the housing is located in a targeted area of economic distress, (2) at least one of the two units is occupied as the principal residence of the mortgagor, and (3) the family income of the mortgagor is 140% or less of the applicable area median family income.

28% WITHHOLDING RATE ON BONUSES

Until the new law takes effect, Treasury regulations provide a 20% withholding rate for bonuses, commissions, and overtime pay. Last year Congress decided that the rate should be increased to 28% where such payments are not included in a regular salary payment, but President Bush vetoed the increase.

New tax law. After 1993, the withholding rate on separately paid bonuses and supplemental wages will increase to 28%. The IRS will specify withholding procedures that will explain how the new rate applies. At the time of this writing, no such procedures had yet been specified.

TOP ESTATE AND GIFT RATES RESTORED

A unified graduated tax rate schedule applies to both estate and gift taxes.

The estate tax is technically an excise tax on the transfer of property on a person's death. For practical purposes you should consider it as the potential tax imposed on the market value of your property at the date of death.

The gift tax is imposed to prevent you from avoiding estate tax by giving away your property before you die. To illustrate with an extreme example, if today you were to give away all your property, the gift tax would be approximately the same as the estate tax imposed on your estate if you died today without giving away the property. However, you can reduce or avoid estate and/or gift taxes by taking advantage of gift and estate tax plans.

Prior law rates. For taxable transfers after 1992, the top rate was reduced to 50% on transfers exceeding $2.5 million. Before 1993, a 53% rate applied to transfers exceeding $2.5 million and below $3 million, and the top rate was 55% on transfers over $3 million.

New tax rates. The top 50% rate is replaced by reinstating the 53% and 55% graduated rates that were in effect before 1993.

The estate and gift tax rates are reduced by certain credits as under prior law.

Prior phaseout rules. For transfers after 1992, the benefits of graduated rates and the unified credit were phased out at a 5% rate for taxable transfers exceeding $10 million but not over $18.34 million.

New range. The phaseout range of $10 million to $21.04 million of prior years is reinstated.

Generation-skipping transfers. Transfers that "skip" a generation, such as a gift to a grandchild, are subject to a special tax if they exceed a lifetime exemption of $1 million per transferor. The calculation of the tax is complicated and partly based on federal estate tax modified by certain ratios. Under prior law, the resulting base was subject to a rate of

50%. Under the new tax law, an earlier higher rate of 55% is restored for transfers after 1992.

LUXURY TAX CUT BACK

The luxury tax is repealed retroactively to the start of 1993 for boats, aircraft, jewelry, and fur. However, the excise tax was kept for automobiles. The threshold of $30,000 is increased to $32,000 for sales after 1993, and is subject to annual inflation adjustments. The cost of special equipment to assist the disabled in driving a car, other than normal accessories such as power steering, power windows or brakes, is not treated as part of the car's cost for purposes of the luxury tax.

Refunds. If you paid a luxury tax in 1993 for a boat, airplane, jewelry or fur, you get a refund of the tax from the seller, who in turn will be refunded by the government.

3
TAXES ON SOCIAL SECURITY BENEFITS

NEW THRESHOLDS FOR FIGURING TAXABLE SOCIAL SECURITY BENEFITS

For 1993 and prior years, all Social Security benefits are tax free if adjusted gross income plus tax-exempt interest and 50% of benefits is below the base amount of $25,000 for single persons, heads of households, or qualifying widow(er)s, or $32,000 for married persons filing a joint return. Married persons who file separately and live together at any time during the year are not allowed any base amount. If adjusted gross income plus tax-exempt interest and 50% of benefits exceeds the base amount, up to 50% of Social Security benefits may be taxable.

New tax law. Starting in 1994, the new law increases the amount of Social Security benefits subject to tax, but only for individuals with incomes above a new $34,000 or $44,000 threshold. The rules do not change for those whose adjusted gross income, plus tax-exempt interest and 50% of Social Security, is below the new threshold of $34,000 for singles, heads of households, and qualifying widow(er)s, and $44,000 for married persons filing jointly. For such persons, the prior law rules for figuring taxable benefits will still apply. That is, no benefits at all are subject to tax if income is below the pre-1994 thresholds of $25,000 or $32,000. No more than 50% of benefits are subject to tax on a joint return if income is over $32,000 and up to $44,000, or for singles, heads of households, and qualifying widow(er)s if income is over $25,000 and up to $34,000.

If income exceeds the new $34,000 or $44,000 threshold, the computation is more complicated, with the maximum amount of taxable benefits limited to 85%. The 85% limit applies if it is less than the following total: (1) 85% of the excess of income over the $34,000 or $44,000 base, plus (2) the lesser of (a) benefits subject to tax under the prior law rules, or (b) $6,000 for married persons filing jointly, or $4,500 for singles, heads of households, or qualifying widow(er)s.

The following worksheets will help you estimate how much of your Social Security benefits will be taxable in 1994.

WORKSHEET 1:

1. **Adjusted gross income (AGI)**			$______
2. *Plus:*	Tax-exempt interest	______	
	Tax-free foreign income	______	
	Tax-free interest on savings bonds used to pay tuition	______	______
3. Modified adjusted gross income (line 1 plus line 2)			______
4. *Plus:* 50% of ______ net Social Security benefits			______
5. **Provisional income** (line 3 plus line 4)			$______

If single and line 5 is:	*Do this:*
* Under $25,000	Stop. None of your benefits will be taxed.
* Between $25,000 and $34,000	Use Worksheet 2 to figure taxable benefits
* Over $34,000	Use Worksheets 2 and 3 to figure taxable benefits

If married filing jointly and line 5 is:	*Do this:*
* Under $32,000	Stop. None of your benefits will be taxed.
* Between $32,000 and $44,000	Use Worksheet 2 to figure taxable benefits
* Over $44,000	Use Worksheets 2 and 4 to figure taxable benefits

If married filing separately and you live together with your spouse at any time during the year, you do not qualify for any base amount. You are taxed on

85% of net Social Security benefits, or if lower, 85% of provisional income.

If married filing separately and you live apart from your spouse for the entire year, follow the rules for single persons; the $25,000 or $34,000 base applies.

WORKSHEET 2: Complete this worksheet if your provisional income (line 5 from Worksheet 1) exceeds $25,000 (single) or $32,000 (married filing jointly).

1. Line 5 from Worksheet 1 (provisional income)	$______
2. Enter $25,000 if single; $32,000 if married filing jointly	______
3. Line 1 less line 2	______
4. 50% of line 3	______
5. Line 4 from Worksheet 1 (50% of net Social Security benefits)	______
6. Lesser of line 4 or line 5	$______

If your provisional income (line 1) does not exceed $34,000 (single) or $44,000 (married filing jointly), line 6 shows the amount of your taxable Social Security benefits.

If your provisional income (line 1) exceeds $34,000 and you are single, go on to Worksheet 3.

If your provisional income (line 1) exceeds $44,000 and you are married filing jointly, go on to Worksheet 4.

WORKSHEET 3: Complete this worksheet if your provisional income (line 1 from Worksheet 2) exceeds $34,000 and you are single.

1. **Provisional income** (line 1 from Worksheet 2)	$_______
2. Adjusted base for single persons	34,000
3. Line 1 less line 2	_______
4. 85% of line 3	_______
5. Line 6 from Worksheet 2	_______
6. Statutory addition for single persons	4,500
7. Lesser of line 5 or line 6	_______
8. Total of line 4 plus line 7	_______
9. 85% of net Social Security benefits	_______
10. **Taxable Social Security benefits:** Lesser of line 8 or line 9	$_______

WORKSHEET 4: Complete this worksheet if your provisional income (line 1 from Worksheet 2) exceeds $44,000 and you are married filing jointly.

1. **Provisional income** (line 1 from Worksheet 2)	$_______
2. Adjusted base for married persons filing jointly	44,000
3. Line 1 less line 2	_______
4. 85% of line 3	_______
5. Line 6 from Worksheet 2	_______
6. Statutory addition for married persons filing jointly	6,000
7. Lesser of line 5 or line 6	_______
8. Total of line 4 plus line 7	_______
9. 85% of net Social Security benefits	_______
10. **Taxable Social Security benefits:** Lesser of line 8 or line 9	$_______

Examples

1. You are single and report an adjusted gross income of $29,000 in 1994. You have also earned $2,000 in tax-exempt interest and receive $10,000 in net Social Security benefits.

WORKSHEET 1:

1. **Adjusted gross income (AGI)**	$29,000
2. Tax-exempt interest	2,000
3. Modified adjusted gross income	$31,000
4. 50% of net Social Security benefits	5,000
5. **Provisional income**	$36,000

Next, use Worksheet 2.

WORKSHEET 2:

1. **Provisional income** (line 5 from Worksheet 1)	$36,000
2. Base amount for single persons	25,000
3. Line 1 less line 2	11,000
4. 50% of line 3	5,500
5. 50% of net Social Security benefits	5,000
6. Lesser of line 4 or line 5	5,000

Because you are single and your provisional income (line 1 from Worksheet 2) exceeds $34,000, you must also complete Worksheet 3 to figure the amount of your taxable Social Security benefits.

WORKSHEET 3:

1. **Provisional income** (line 1 from Worksheet 2)	$36,000
2. Adjusted base for single persons	34,000
3. Line 1 less line 2	2,000
4. 85% of line 3	1,700
5. Line 6 from Worksheet 2	5,000
6. Statutory addition for single persons	4,500
7. Lesser of line 5 or line 6	4,500
8. Total of line 4 plus line 7	6,200
9. 85% of net Social Security benefits (85% of $10,000)	8,500
10. **Taxable Social Security benefits:** Lesser of line 8 or line 9	6,200

2. You are married and on a 1994 joint return report adjusted gross income of $50,000, tax-exempt interest of $3,000, and net Social Security benefits of $19,000.

WORKSHEET 1:

1. **Adjusted gross income (AGI)**	$50,000
2. Tax-exempt interest	3,000
3. Modified adjusted gross income	$53,000
4. 50% of net Social Security benefits	9,500
5. **Provisional income**	$62,500

Next, use Worksheet 2.

WORKSHEET 2:

1. **Provisional income** (line 5 from Worksheet 1)	$62,500
2. Base amount for married persons filing jointly	32,000
3. Line 1 less line 2	30,500
4. 50% of line 3	15,250
5. 50% of net Social Security benefits	9,500
6. Lesser of line 4 or line 5	9,500

Because you are married filing jointly and your provisional income (line 1 from Worksheet 2) exceeds $44,000, you must also complete Worksheet 4 to figure the amount of your taxable Social Security benefits.

WORKSHEET 4:

1. **Provisional income** (line 1 from Worksheet 2)	$62,500
2. Adjusted base for married persons filing jointly	44,000
3. Line 1 less line 2	18,500
4. 85% of line 3	15,725
5. Line 6 from Worksheet 2	9,500
6. Statutory addition for married persons filing jointly	6,000
7. Lesser of line 5 or line 6	6,000
8. Total of line 4 plus line 7	21,725
9. 85% of net Social Security benefits	16,150
10. **Taxable Social Security benefits:** Lesser of line 8 or line 9	$16,150

SOCIAL SECURITY BENEFITS SUBJECT TO TAX

If you receive Social Security benefits in 1993, you should receive Form SSA-1099 by January 31, 1994. The form will show the total of paid or repaid benefits. Amounts withheld for Medicare premiums, worker's compensation offset, or attorney's fees are itemized and included in the total benefits you received. Keep Form SSA-1099 for your records; do not attach it to your return.

The *net benefit* shown on Form SSA-1099 (benefits paid less benefits repaid) is the benefit amount used to determine taxable benefits.

Railroad Retirement benefits. The portion of your Tier 1 Railroad Retirement Benefits that is equivalent to Social Security retirement benefits is subject to tax as if it were Social Security benefits. If any part of your 1993 Tier 1 benefits is equivalent to Social Security benefits, you should receive Form RRB-1099 from the government by January 31, 1994. The *net* Social Security Equivalent Benefit shown on Form RRB-1099 is the amount used to determine taxable benefits. Other Tier 1 Railroad Retirement benefits, as well as Tier 2 benefits, are treated as pension income and not as Social Security benefits subject to tax.

Benefits paid on behalf of child or incompetent. If a child is entitled to Social Security benefits, such as after the death of a parent, the benefit is considered to be the child's regardless of who actually receives the payment. Whether the child's benefit is subject to tax will depend on the amount of the child's income reported on the child's tax return.

Workers' compensation. If you are receiving Social Security disability payments and workers' compensation for the same disability, your Social Security benefits may be reduced by the workers' compensation. For example, you are entitled to Social Security disability benefits of $5,000 a year. After receiving a $1,000 workers' compensation award, your disability benefits are reduced to $4,000. You treat the full $5,000 as Social Security benefits, which may be subject to tax.

Repayment of benefits. If you forfeit part of your Social Security benefits because of excessive outside income, the forfeited amount reduces your benefits for purposes of the computation of taxable benefits. You make the reduction even if the forfeit relates to benefits received in a prior year. For example, your regular 1993 benefit of $5,000 is reduced by $1,000 because of earnings of the prior year. For tax purposes, your 1993 benefits are considered $4,000.

If in 1992, Social Security benefits were subject to tax, and in 1993, you repaid 1992 benefits that were taxed, the repayment will be reflected in the *net benefit* shown on Form SSA-1099. If the repayment exceeds 1993 benefits, you may claim the excess as a miscellaneous itemized deduction or as a credit, depending on the amount of the repayment.

ELECTION FOR LUMP-SUM SOCIAL SECURITY BENEFIT PAYMENT

If you receive a lump-sum payment of benefits covering prior years, you have a choice: (1) You may treat the entire payment as a benefit taxable in the year of payment, or (2) you may allocate the benefits over the taxable years in which they were payable.

Choose the method that provides the lowest required increase to income in the current year. This rule may be to your advantage if you receive a lump-sum benefit in 1994 that is attributable to 1993. If the amount is subject to the 85% inclusion rule, you will elect to treat the 1993 portion of the benefit as payable in 1993 and taxable under the 50% inclusion rule.

When you elect to allocate benefits to a prior year, you do not amend the return for that year. You compute the increase in income (if any) that would have resulted if the Social Security benefits had been received in that year. You then add that amount to the income of the current year.

TAX ON BENEFITS REDUCES SUPPLEMENTAL EARNINGS

If you are working to supplement your income, consider the added tax cost of earning income which subjects your Social Security benefits to tax. You have to figure not only the tax on the extra income but also the tax on the Social Security benefits treated as taxable income. The marginal tax rate on the extra income will be higher than the regular rates. This penalty exists even if extra earnings subject only 50% of Social Security benefits to tax. The effective tax on additional earnings figured at 50% in the 15% bracket is 22.5%. It is even greater where 85% of benefits is included. If you are in the 28% bracket, the effective rate on such earnings subject to an 85% inclusion may be 51.8%.

4
PERSONAL AND JOB-RELATED DEDUCTIONS

RECEIPTS NEEDED TO SUPPORT DONATIONS OF $250 OR MORE

If you make a cash donation in 1993 to a qualifying charity, you may rely on a cancelled check to support your contribution. However, checks to charities can sometimes cover not only donations but also goods or services received from the charity. For example, at an art auction to raise funds for a charity, a check made out to the charity might in large part represent the price of an art item; only a portion might actually be a donation. To eliminate the temptation to claim such transactions entirely as charitable donations, after 1993 all separate donations of $250 or more must be evidenced by a written receipt or statement from the charity.

New tax law. Starting in 1994, no deduction will be allowed for a separate donation of $250 or more unless you have a written statement from the charity as a receipt. If you received any goods or services for a payment, the statement must provide an estimate of the value of whatever you received. Even where no consideration is given for the donation, the receipt must state that fact.

The law does not impose a reporting requirement on the charity. You are responsible for asking for a receipt before filing a return on which your contribution is claimed as a deduction. A receipt or acknowledgment may be made by letter, postcard, or computer-generated form. Further, a donee organization may prepare a separate acknowledgment for each donation or may provide donors with periodic annual acknowledgments for donations of $250 or more received during the year.

Where a charity files a return reporting the amount of your deductible contribution, you may not need a receipt. However, the IRS has yet to clarify exactly how you may take advantage of this procedure.

Separate payments made at different times during the year for fund-raising events generally will not be aggregated. However, the IRS has been instructed to write anti-abuse rules to prevent evasion of the disclosure requirement through the issuance of multiple checks on the same date.

Contributions made through wage withholding plans are treated as separate contributions and are not aggregated.

Intangible "religious benefits," such as pew seating reservations, are not considered as goods or services that must be valued. However, a receipt from a religious organization must state that a religious benefit was furnished.

If a contribution exceeds $75 but is less than $250, a written receipt is not required, but the charity must still inform the donor how to reduce the deduction if quid pro quo goods or services have been received, unless the only benefits are intangible religious benefits.

DISASTER RELIEF FOR HOMEOWNERS AND RENTERS

The new tax law gives several tax breaks to certain individuals whose homes have been damaged as a result of natural disasters, or who have suffered property damage to the contents of their homes as a result of such disasters. These tax breaks are available only in regard to property in locations designated as disaster areas by the President on or after September 1, 1991.

First, insurance proceeds for unscheduled personal property (under homeowner or renter policies) in the home will be disregarded for tax purposes. Thus any gain realized on the reimbursement will not be taxed. Further, the period allowed for buying a new home in order to defer tax on gains realized from insurance proceeds is extended from two to four years. Finally, when replacing a home, insurance proceeds for the old home and its contents are treated as insurance for a single property, and thus may be invested in a new home or contents in any proportion.

HEALTH INSURANCE DEDUCTION FOR SELF-EMPLOYED

Before the new tax law was passed, health insurance costs of self-employed persons were partly tax-deductible only if paid before July 1, 1992. The new law reinstates the deduction as of that date.

If you are self-employed, you may deduct 25% of the cost of health coverage for yourself, your spouse, and dependents. The deduction may not exceed your net earnings from the business for which the health plan is established.

You may not claim the deduction for any month that you have employee coverage under another plan or coverage under your spouse's employer's plan. The deduction is allowed as an adjustment to income on line 26 of Form 1040 whether or not you claim itemized deductions. If itemized deductions are claimed, the remaining 75% of insurance costs and premium costs are deductible as a medical expense, subject to the 7.5% adjusted gross income floor. S corporation shareholders owning more than 2% of the stock may claim the 25% deduction subject to the same limitations.

Under the new law, for premiums paid in 1992 after June 30, you may file an amended 1992 return claiming a deduction of 25% of such premium costs. Use Form 1040X to claim the refund.

For premiums paid in 1993, the deduction may be claimed on a 1993 tax return.

The status of the deduction after 1993 is not clear. The current reinstatement expires after 1993. The comprehensive health plan bill expected in the near future may allow a full deduction of health insurance premiums.

MOVING EXPENSES TO A NEW JOB LOCATION

Qualifying unreimbursed moving expenses to a new job location are deductible for 1993 if you claim itemized deductions. If you do not itemize, you may not deduct any moving expenses. You may decide not to itemize when the standard deduction exceeds the total of your itemized deductions including the deductible moving expenses.

Moving expenses are not reduced by the 2% AGI floor.

To deduct moving expenses, under the 1993 rules, you were required to meet a 35-mile distance test and a time test for remaining in the area of the new job: 39 weeks if an employee or 78 weeks if self-employed.

Moving expenses qualifying for deduction were as follows.

- Moving household goods
- Travel, meals and lodging to transport the taxpayer and family
- Travel, meals and lodging for househunting trips
- Meals and temporary lodging for up to 30 days near the new job location
- Selling (or settling an existing lease on) the old residence and buying (or acquiring a lease on) the new residence

The moving expense deduction was subject to certain dollar limitations. The deduction for househunting and temporary quarters could not exceed $1,500. The deduction for selling, buying and settling leases could not exceed $3,000 less the amount claimed for househunting and temporary quarters.

New tax law. The rules for moving expenses incurred after 1993 are substantially revised. The distance test for a qualifying move is increased from 35 to 50 miles.

The deduction will include only the costs of moving household goods and personal effects, and the costs of travel to the new residence—but not meals.

No deduction will be allowed for pre-move househunting trips, temporary living expenses or expenses of selling, purchasing, or leasing the old or new residence.

Unreimbursed expenses that qualify for the deduction will be deductible from gross income in computing adjusted gross income. This means that if you do not itemize deductions on Schedule A but instead claim the standard deduction, you may deduct moving costs on page 1 of Form 1040.

Reimbursements of moving costs that qualify for the deduction will not be treated as taxable pay but as a tax-free fringe benefit. Under prior law, all reimbursements were treated as pay.

Reimbursements of nonqualifying moving costs will be taxable as pay.

REDUCTION OF BUSINESS MEAL AND ENTERTAINMENT COST BASE

Prior law. Under prior law, you could deduct 80% of unreimbursed expenses incurred in entertaining customers or clients at home or at restaurants, country clubs, theaters, and sporting events. That 80% balance was reduced by the 2% adjusted gross income floor if you were an employee.

New tax law. After 1993, the deduction ceiling is reduced from 80% to 50%.

For example, say that you incur—and pay—unreimbursed business meal costs of $2,000. If you pay those costs in 1993, $1,600 ($2,000 times 80%) of the costs may be deductible. If you pay those costs in 1994, however, only $1,000 ($2,000 times 50%) may be deductible.

All entertainment costs, including meals, must be backed up with records. If you do not keep adequate records, your deductions will be disallowed. You must be prepared to show that meal and entertainment costs are ordinary and necessary to your business; and also:

- Directly related to the active conduct of your business, or
- Directly preceding or following a substantial and bona fide business discussion on a subject associated with the active conduct of your business. This test applies to dining and entertainment in which you seek new business or to goodwill entertainment to encourage the continuation of an existing business relationship. Under this test, you may entertain business associates in nonbusiness settings such as restaurants, theaters, sports arenas, and nightclubs, provided the entertainment directly precedes or follows the business discussion. Business associates are: established or prospective customers, clients, suppliers, employees, agents, partners, or professional advisers, whether established or prospective.

The directly related test limits the deduction of dining and entertainment costs at restaurants, nightclubs, on yachts, at sporting events, on hunting trips, and during social events. If such dining or entertainment fails to meet the directly related test, it may qualify under the rules which require the holding of a business discussion before or after the entertainment. The directly related test may be met in one of these three ways: (1) under the generally related test; (2) as expenses incurred in a clear business setting; or (3) as expenses incurred for services performed.

Generally related test. Under this test, you must show a business motive for the dining or entertainment and business activity during the entertainment. You must show that you had more than a general expectation of getting future income or other specific business benefit (other than goodwill). Although you do not have to prove that income or other business benefit actually resulted from the expense, such evidence will help support your claim. What type of business activity will an IRS agent look for? The agent will seek proof that a business meeting, negotiation, or discussion took place during the period of dining or entertainment. It is not necessary that more time be devoted to business than to entertainment. What if you did not talk business? You must prove that you would have done so except for reasons beyond your control.

Expenses incurred in a clear business setting meet the directly related test provided also that you had no significant motive for incurring the expenses other than to further your business. Entertainment of people with whom you have no personal or social relationship is usually considered to have occurred in a clear business setting. For example, entertaining business representatives and civic leaders at the opening of a new hotel or theatrical production to obtain business publicity rather than goodwill is considered to be entertainment in a clear business setting. Also, entertainment which involves a price rebate is considered to have occurred in a clear business setting, as, for example, when a hotel owner provides occasional free dinners at the hotel for a customer who patronizes the hotel.

Costs of a hospitality room displaying company products at a convention are also a directly related expense.

Taxes and tips are considered part of the cost subject to the 80% or 50% limit. If your employer reimburses your expenses, the limit applies to the employer.

The 80% or 50% limit applies to both employees and the self-employed. It also applies to the IRS meal allowance deduction. The limit is taken into account on Form 2106 for employee expenses, and on Schedule C for self-employment expenses.

Example: In 1994, you pay meal and entertainment costs of \$5,000. Only \$2,500 (\$5,000 times 50%) will be considered deductible. Suppose, however, that your employer reimburses your costs after you account for the expenses. Your employer's deduction is limited to \$2,500. You have no deduction.

CLUB DUES

Under prior law, dues for a country club or any other social, athletic, or sporting club were deductible if certain rules and regulations were met. These requirements were as follows.

You first had to show that you used the club more than 50% of the time during the year to further your business. But this percentage of use did not give you the measure of the deduction of club dues. You also had to show how much of the use of the club was for entertainment directly related to the active conduct of your business. This percentage of directly related entertainment fixed the amount of your club dues deduction. That meant that goodwill entertainment could be counted in determining if you could deduct any club dues at all. But the actual amount of dues to be deducted was based on entertainment directly related to your business and did not include goodwill entertainment.

In making this allocation, you included the cost of your own meals as part of the cost of directly related entertainment.

New tax law. Under the new tax law, this deduction—along with all of these complicated rules and regulations—is junked. After 1993, no deduction will be allowed for club dues, including social, athletic, luncheon, and sporting clubs. However, specific business expenses incurred at a club, such as business meal costs, would be deductible subject to the 50% reduction.

TRAVEL COSTS FOR SPOUSES

Prior law. Prior IRS guidelines made it difficult to justify a deduction for a spouse's expenses on a business trip. Generally, the IRS assumed that a spouse's presence was for personal reasons, and would disallow a deduction for the spouse's travel expenses. However, if a bona fide business purpose could be shown for a spouse's presence on a trip, a deduction might have been allowed.

New tax law. The new law imposes a new restriction, effective in 1994, on deduction of a spouse's travel expenses. Under the new rule, a travel expense deduction for a spouse, dependent, or any other individual accompanying you on a business trip will be denied unless that person is your employee and there is a bona fide business purpose for his or her presence.

5
BUSINESS TAX CHANGES

HIGHER TAX RATE FOR CORPORATIONS

The corporate tax increase is directed at the most highly profitable corporations. Only corporations with taxable incomes over $10 million are affected.

Prior law. Under prior law, there were three corporate tax rates: 15% on the first $50,000 of taxable income, 25% on taxable income between $50,000 and $75,000, and a top rate of 34% for taxable income that exceeded $75,000. For corporations with taxable income in excess of $100,000, the benefit of the 15% and 25% brackets was phased out under a recapture rule that increased the tax liability of the corporation by the lesser of (1) 5% of the excess of taxable income over $100,000, or (2) $11,750.

New tax law. The new maximum tax rate for corporations is 35%. It applies to corporate taxable incomes in excess of $10 million. A corporation with taxable income over $15 million also must increase its tax liability by the lesser of (1) 3% of the excess of income over $15 million, or (2) $100,000. This has the effect of setting a 38% rate for taxable income between $15 million and $18,333,333.

The new rates apply retroactively to taxable years starting on or after January 1, 1993. However, estimated tax penalties are not imposed for the 1993 tax year to the extent that the increased rate was not used in making corporate estimated tax payments.

The tax rate for personal service corporations increases from 34% to 35%.

Fiscal-year corporations will apply a blended tax rate for fiscal years starting in 1992 and ending after January 1, 1993.

The table on page 77 lists the new corporate tax rates.

Corporate tax rates

If taxable income is:		The tax is:	
Over—	But not over—		Of the amount over—
$ 0	$ 50,000	15%	$ 0
50,000	75,000	25%	50,000
75,000*	10,000,000	34%	75,000
$10,000,000**	—	35%	$10,000,000

*Where taxable income exceeds $100,000, the tax is increased by the lesser of (1) 5% of the excess or (2) $11,750.
**Where taxable income exceeds $15,000,000, the tax is increased by the lesser of (1) 3% of the excess or (2) $100,000.

ESTIMATED TAX RULES FOR CORPORATIONS

For tax years beginning prior to December 31, 1993, corporations have been required to make four timely estimated tax payments to the IRS to avoid a penalty. The estimated payments generally have had to be based on 97% of the corporation's projected current-year tax liability under an annualized income method. However, under an exception, smaller corporations that did not have taxable income of $1 million or more over three prior taxable years could avoid a penalty by paying 100% of the prior year's liability in four equal installments. A large corporation with taxable income over $1 million in any of the three preceding years could take advantage of the 100% prior-year tax rule only in determining its first quarterly payment.

New tax law. Starting for years beginning after December 31, 1993, a corporation must base quarterly estimated tax payments on 100% of the current tax liability under either the actual or annualized basis. However, it may still take advantage of the exception allowing payments to be based on 100% of the prior year's tax liability as described above.

New annualized income elections are also introduced by the new law.

INCENTIVES FOR INVESTMENTS IN EMPOWERMENT ZONES AND ENTERPRISE COMMUNITIES

The 1992 civil disturbances in Los Angeles spurred Congress to consider a system of tax and financial incentives to encourage businesses to operate in distressed urban and rural areas. The first concrete step is a law authorizing nine empowerment zones and 95 enterprise communities in 1994 and 1995.

Special financing is offered for businesses in both empowerment zones and enterprise communities. In addition, businesses in empowerment zones get these two tax incentives:

- a 20% tax credit for the first $15,000 of qualified wages paid to an eligible employee who lives in the zone; the maximum credit is $3,000 per year for each employee
- an extra first-year expensing deduction of $20,000

To qualify as an empowerment zone, an area must have a condition of pervasive poverty, unemployment, and general economic distress which may include distress from a high incidence of crime and narcotics abuse. Under the new law, six empowerment zones and 65 enterprise communities will be located in eligible urban areas and three empowerment zones and 30 enterprise communities will be located in rural areas.

The enterprise areas are designated only from areas nominated by state and local governments. They must also meet criteria such as having a minimum population and maximum size, conditions of unemployment and general economic distress, and poverty rates of generally 25% or more. The state and local governments have to adopt a specific course of action designed to reduce burdens on employers and to improve the community for residents.

No area may be designated as an empowerment zone or an enterprise community unless the nominating state or local government provides written assurances that its strategic plan will be implemented.

General distress for a zone may be indicated by factors such as high crime rates, high vacancy rates, or designation of an area as a disaster area or high-intensity drug trafficking area ("HIDTA") under the Anti-Drug Abuse Act of 1988; job loss (including manufacturing job loss); and economic distress due to closures of military bases or restrictions on timber harvesting. In addition, consideration will be given to communities along the U.S. border in which population has increased significantly and in which a significant portion of the area's population resides in substandard housing.

The Department of Housing and Urban Development is responsible for designating empowerment zones and enterprise communities.

Employer wage credit. A 20% credit against income tax liability is allowed to employers in an empowerment zone for the first $15,000 of qualified wages paid to each employee who is a zone resident and performs substantially all employment services within the zone in the business of the employer.

The maximum credit per qualified employee is $3,000 per year. Where wages paid to a qualified employee exceed $15,000, only the first $15,000 of wages is eligible for the credit. The wage credit is allowed regardless of the number of other employees who work for the employer.

The credit will be phased out beginning in 2002; it will be 15% in 2002, 10% in 2003, and 5% in 2004. The credit will expire after December 31, 2004.

Qualified wages include the first $15,000 of salary and wages and certain training and educational expenses paid for the employee, provided that the expenses are paid to an unrelated third party and are tax free, or in the case of an employee under age 19, the expenses are incurred by the employer in operating a youth training program with local education officials.

The credit covers both full-time and part-time employees. However, an employee must work a minimum period of at least 90 days. The credit does not cover pay to relatives or related owners of the employer.

The tax deduction for wages is reduced by the amount of credit claimed. The credit may also offset up to 25% of alternative minimum tax liability.

A business in an empowerment zone may also claim a first-year expense deduction for depreciable business equipment of up to $37,500. Investments in buildings do not qualify for the deduction.

The expensing deduction will be recaptured if the property is not used predominantly in an enterprise zone business.

Financing investments through issues of tax-exempt facility bonds will be available for both business empowerment zones and enterprise communities.

Separate tax incentives are provided for businesses located in Indian reservations.

FIRST-YEAR EXPENSING DEDUCTION INCREASED

You may elect to deduct a certain amount (up to $10,000 under prior law) of the cost of certain business equipment in the year you place it in service. The election is limited to tangible personal property bought for business use, such as machinery, office equipment, a computer, a car, or a truck acquired from non-related parties. The deduction is not allowed for buildings, structural components of buildings, furniture or refrigerators used in operating apartment buildings, property held for the production of income, or equipment previously used for personal purposes, such as an automobile bought for pleasure but later used for business. The portion of cost not eligible for first-year expensing may be recovered by depreciation under the regular MACRS depreciation rules. The first-year expensing deduction is technically called "the Section 179 deduction."

You elect the first-year expensing deduction on

Form 4562, which you attach to your Form 1040. You may not revoke the expensing election without IRS consent.

New tax law. You may now deduct up to $17,500 for equipment placed in service in 1993 and later years. For fiscal-year businesses, the increased deduction applies to tax years starting after 1992. Businesses in empowerment zones may deduct up to $37,500 starting in 1994.

The top expensing deduction for an automobile placed in service in 1993 is $2,860 because of the special "luxury car" limit placed on depreciation deductions for automobiles.

RESEARCH AND EXPERIMENTATION CREDIT EXTENDED

The new law extends the 20% research tax credit retroactively from July 1, 1992, until June 30, 1995. The credit applies to 20% of the qualifying research expenses in excess of a historic base amount. Technical rules apply for determining eligibility for and computation of the credit. In general, the expenses qualifying for the credit are wages and supplies used in research conducted in the United States,

65% of amounts paid for contract research conducted on the taxpayer's behalf, and certain time-sharing costs of computer use in research. The credit does not apply to research in the social sciences, arts, or humanities or any research subsidized by government or other persons.

Special credit computation rules apply to start-up companies and to research expenses of university and tax-exempt scientific research organizations.

There is also a new rule for determining the base amount of start-up companies. A taxpayer that did not have gross receipts in at least three years during the 1984–1988 period may be assigned a fixed base percentage of 3% for each of its first five taxable years after 1993 in which it incurs qualified research expenditures. The fixed base percentage for the sixth through tenth taxable years after 1993 in which qualified research expenditures are incurred is as follows: (1) for the sixth year, one-sixth of the ratio of qualified research expenditures to gross receipts for the fourth and fifth years; (2) for the seventh year, one-third of the fifth and sixth years; (3) for the eighth year, one-half of the ratio for the fifth through seventh years; (4) for the ninth year, two-thirds of the ratio for the fifth through eighth years; and (5) for the tenth year, five-sixths of the ratio for the fifth through ninth years. For later years, the fixed base percentage will be the actual ratio of qualified research expenditures to gross receipts for five years selected by the taxpayer from the fifth through tenth taxable years.

TARGETED JOB CREDIT EXTENDED

Until it expired on June 30, 1992, the targeted jobs credit gave a tax credit to employers who hired individuals in nine designated categories. The new tax law extends the tax credit retroactively for 30 months until December 31, 1994, thereby continuing the incentive for employers to hire workers who might otherwise find it difficult to obtain employment.

Employers who hire individuals in the following categories may claim the credit retroactively for workers who began work for the employer after June 30, 1992. The targeted groups are: (1) vocational rehabilitation referrals: (2) economically disadvantaged youths aged 18 through 22; (3) economically disadvantaged Vietnam-era veterans; (4) Supplemental Security Income (SSI) recipients; (5) general assistance recipients; (6) economically disadvantaged cooperative education students aged 16 through 19; (7) economically disadvantaged ex-convicts; (8) eligible work incentive employees; and (9) economically disadvantaged summer youth employees aged 16 or 17. Certification of targeted group membership is required as a condition of claiming the credit.

For employees in the targeted groups, the amount of the tax credit is generally equal to 40% of the first

$6,000 of qualified first-year wages. Thus, the maximum credit generally is $2,400 per individual. With respect to economically disadvantaged summer youth employees, however, the credit is equal to 40% of up to $3,000 of wages, for a maximum credit of $1,200. The credit is not available for wages paid to a targeted group member unless the individual either (1) is employed by the employer for at least 90 days or 14 days in the case of economically disadvantaged summer youth employees; *or* (2) has completed at least 120 hours of work performed for the employer, 20 hours in the case of economically disadvantaged summer youth employees. The employer's deduction for wages must be reduced by the amount of the credit claimed.

CAP ON HIGH-EARNER RETIREMENT CONTRIBUTIONS

Company retirement plans such as 401(k) plans and profit-sharing plans, as well as Keogh plans for the self-employed, are subject to nondiscriminatory tests to assure that benefits are not unreasonably skewed in favor of highly compensated employees. Another means of limiting retirement plan contributions and benefits for higher-paid executives and owner-employees is the annual limit on compensation that the plan can take into account. Under prior law, that limit was $235,840. If an employee receives compensation in excess of the limit, the excess compensation cannot be used to determine the amount of the employee's benefit or allocation under the plan.

New tax law. The annual limit of $235,840 is cut back to $150,000 for plan years starting after 1993. The cutback does not result in any reduction of benefits already accrued because the reduced limit applies only to compensation for 1994 and thereafter, and does not limit compensation for prior years that has been taken into account for determining benefits.

Special provisions modify the effect of the cutback for state and local government plans and for plans negotiated under a collective bargaining agreement.

PARTNERSHIP LIQUIDATION DISTRIBUTIONS

Prior law. Under prior law, a partnership could treat payments to a withdrawing partner for unrealized receivables and goodwill as a distributive share or guaranteed payments and so deduct part of the distribution.

New tax law. Under the new law, distributions on liquidation of a partner's interest attributed to unrealized receivables and goodwill are treated as made in exchange for the partner's interest in the partnership. This treatment prevents an ordinary deduction for amounts attributed to the distribution. A payment covering depreciation recapture is also treated as made in exchange for the partner's partnership interest.

The new rule does not apply to payments to a general partner of a partnership in which capital is not a material income-producing factor. According to a committee report, capital is not a material income-producing factor if substantially all of gross income consists of fees, commissions, or other compensation for personal services. Thus, a professional partnership of doctors, dentists, lawyers, architects or accountants is not treated as a business in which capital is a material income-producing factor, even though substantial capital investments may be made in professional or office equipment.

The new rule also does not affect a deduction claimed for compensation paid to a retiring partner for past services.

Unbilled amounts are not considered unrealized receivables.

Effective date. The new rule applies to partners

retiring or dying on or after January 5, 1993. It does not apply to partners retiring on or after January 5, 1993, if a written contract to purchase the partner's interest was binding on January 4, 1993, and at all times thereafter before such purchase.

PARTNERSHIP DISTRIBUTIONS WHEN THE PARTNERSHIP OWNS APPRECIATED PROPERTY

Amounts received by a partner in exchange for his or her interest in a partnership are treated as ordinary income to the extent attributable to substantially appreciated inventory of the partnership. In addition, distributions by a partnership in which a partner receives substantially appreciated inventory in return for his or her interest in certain other partnership property (or receives certain other property in exchange for substantially appreciated inventory) are treated as a taxable sale or exchange of property rather than as a nontaxable distribution.

Under prior law, inventory in such cases was treated as substantially appreciated if the value of the partnership inventory exceeded both 120% of its adjusted basis and 10% of the value of all partnership property (other than money).

The IRS claimed that the 10% exception created tax avoidance opportunities through the manipulation of the partnership gross assets.

New tax law. The new law repeals the requirement that the partnership inventory must exceed 10% of the value of all partnership property to be considered substantially appreciated. Only the 120% rule remains. Thus if the partnership inventory exceeds 120% of adjusted basis, the inventory is treated as substantially appreciated. In addition, any inventory property acquired with the principal purpose of reducing the appreciation to less than 120% to avoid ordinary income treatment is disregarded in applying the 120% test.

The new law applies to sales, exchanges, and distributions after April 30, 1993.

DEDUCTION CAP ON TOP EXECUTIVE PAY

The IRS imposes a reasonable salary test primarily against closely held corporations, which may try to avoid nondeductible dividend distributions to employee stockholders by paying them high salaries instead. Whether a salary is reasonable and thus deductible depends on these factors:

- Duties performed by the employee
- Volume of business handled
- The character and amount of the employee's responsibility
- The complexities of the business
- The amount of time required
- The cost of living in the community
- Ability and achievements
- The amount of pay in comparison with the corporation's gross and net income

These factors are viewed at the time the contract for services was made, not when the compensation was actually paid or accrued. Often a crucial fact is whether the salary is comparable to salaries received by other executives in similar companies in the industry. Sometimes a record of substantial dividend payments over past years may negate the IRS challenge of reasonable salary.

If the IRS sustains a claim that a salary is not reasonable, the deduction for the salary is disallowed to the corporation and in effect the payment is treated as a dividend payment.

In publicly-held corporations, deductions of large salaries paid to executives have rarely been questioned as "unreasonable." Executives' salaries are generally arrived at by arm's-length bargaining and with no need to disguise dividend distributions as salary. Often the executives are not stockholders.

New tax law. Starting in 1994, the deduction for compensation paid to a top executive of a publicly held company will be limited to $1 million.

A corporation is publicly held if it has a class of common equity securities that must be registered under the Securities Exchange Act of 1934. However, a corporation that registered voluntarily is not considered publicly held.

Affected by the new law are generally the chief executive officer (CEO) at the close of the year and an executive who is considered one of the four highest-compensated officers (excluding the CEO) for the year under SEC reporting rules.

The deduction cap applies to all remuneration for services, including benefits, for which a deduction would otherwise be allowed. However, the following types of compensation are not subject to the cap: commissions based on the executive's personal performance, payments to a tax-qualified retirement plan, amounts excludable from gross income (such as employer-provided health benefits), and remuneration paid under a written contract in effect on February 17, 1993.

The deduction cap also does not apply to pay based on meeting performance goals established by a compensation committee made up of outside directors, when the payment terms and performance goals were disclosed to and approved by the shareholders. The compensation committee also must certify that the performance goals were satisfied.

DEDUCTIONS NOW ALLOWED FOR GOODWILL AND OTHER BOUGHT INTANGIBLES

In the past, the IRS has consistently disallowed amortization deductions for purchased goodwill and intangibles akin to goodwill on the grounds that such assets have no ascertainable useful life. The issue has often been litigated in situations in which business persons have claimed that under the particular facts of the case, useful life can be estimated. Recently, the Supreme Court held that a taxpayer, who can prove that a particular intangible asset can be valued and a limited useful life with reasonable accuracy can also be valued, may depreciate the value over the useful life. However, the Court also recognized that this kind of proof cannot often be successfully presented.

New tax law. For the first time, the new law provides specific statutory authorization for deducting purchased goodwill and other intangibles. The statute covering the subject is Code Section 197, and intangible assets such as goodwill are now dubbed "section 197 intangibles." As such, they are ratably amortizable over a 15-year period starting in the month of acquisition. The 15-year period applies regardless of actual useful life.

A section 197 intangible is amortizable if acquired after August 10, 1993, and held in connection with a business or in an activity engaged in for the production of income.

Generally, the amount subject to amortization is cost.

What are section 197 intangibles? The term "section 197 intangible" is defined as: (1) goodwill; (2) going-concern value; (3) workforce in place; (4) information base; (5) know-how; (6) any customer-based intangible; (7) any supplier-based intangible; (8) any license, permit, or other right granted by a governmental unit or agency; (9) any covenant not to compete made in the acquisition of a business; and (10) any franchise, trademark, or trade name.

Goodwill. Goodwill is defined by a Committee report as the value of a business attributable to the expectancy of continued customer patronage, due to the name or reputation of a business or any other factor.

Going-concern value is defined as the additional value that attaches to property because it is an integral part of a going concern. This includes the value attributable to the ability of a trade or business to continue to operate and generate sales without interruption in spite of a change in ownership.

Workforce in place. The portion of the purchase price of an acquired business attributable to a highly skilled workforce is amortizable over 15 years. Similarly, the cost of acquiring an existing employment contract is amortizable over 15 years.

Information base. This includes the cost of acquiring customer lists; subscription lists; insurance expirations; patient or client files; lists of newspaper, magazine, radio or television advertisers; business books and records; and operating systems. The intangible value of technical manuals, training manuals or programs, data files, and accounting or inventory control systems is also a section 197 intangible.

Know-how. A patent, copyright, formula, process, design, pattern, know-how, format, or similar item is a section 197 intangible. However, the following interests if not acquired in the acquisition of a business are not section 197 intangibles: patents; and interests in films, sound recordings, videotapes, books, or other similar property.

Customer-based intangibles. Customer-based intangibles include the portion of an acquired trade or business attributable to a customer base, circulation base, undeveloped market or market growth, insurance in force, investment management contracts, or other relationships with customers that involve the future provision of goods or services.

Supplier-based intangibles. The portion of the purchase price of an acquired business attributable to a favorable relationship with persons who provide distribution services, such as favorable shelf or display space at a retail outlet, the existence of a favorable credit rating, or the existence of favorable supply contracts are section 197 intangibles.

Covenants not to compete. Excessive compensation or rental paid to a former owner of a business for continuing to perform services or provide the use of property is considered an amount paid for a covenant not to compete if the services or property benefits the trade or business. But an amount paid under a covenant not to compete which actually represents additional consideration for the corporate stock is not a section 197 intangible and must be added to the basis of the acquired stock.

Franchises, trademarks and trade names. A franchise, trademark, or trade name is a section 197 intangible. Amounts, whether fixed or contingent, paid on the transfer of a trademark, trade name, or franchise are chargeable to capital account and must be ratably amortized over a 15-year period. The renewal of a franchise, trademark, or trade name is treated as an acquisition of the franchise, trademark, or trade name. Renewal costs are amortized over 15 years beginning in the month of renewal.

Self-created intangibles. A section 197 intangible created by a taxpayer is generally not amortizable, unless created in connection with a transaction that involves the acquisition of assets of a business. However, this deduction bar for self-created intangibles does not apply to (1) any license, permit, or other right granted by a governmental unit or agency; (2) a covenant not to compete entered into on the acquisition of a business; (3) any franchise, trademark, or trade name. For example, the 15-year amortization period may apply to the capitalized costs of registering or developing a trademark or trade name.

According to a Committee report, a person who contracts for or renews a contract for the use of a section 197 intangible is not considered to have created that intangible. For example, a licensee who contracts for the use of know-how may amortize capitalized costs over 15 years.

The following intangible assets are not section 197 intangibles: (1) interests in a corporation, partnership, trust or estate; (2) interests under certain financial contracts; (3) interests in land; (4) certain computer software; (5) certain separately acquired rights and interests; (6) interests under existing leases of tangible property; (7) interests under existing indebtedness; (8) sports franchises; (9) certain residential mortgage servicing rights; and (10) certain corporate transaction costs.

Computer software. Computer software readily available to the general public is not a section 197 intangible. Computer software is considered a section 197 intangible only if acquired in the acquisition of a business.

Loss limitations. A person who disposes of an

amortizable section 197 intangible at loss and at the same time retains other section 197 intangibles acquired in the same transaction may not deduct the loss. The disallowed loss is added to the basis of the retained section 197 intangibles. The same rule applies if a section 197 intangible is abandoned or becomes worthless and other section 197 intangibles acquired in the same transaction are kept. The basis of the remaining intangibles is increased by the disallowed loss.

You may not treat a covenant not to compete as worthless any earlier than the disposition or worthlessness of the entire interest in a business.

Anti-churning rules. No deduction is allowed for goodwill, going concern value, or any other section 197 intangibles acquired by a taxpayer after August 10, 1993 if:

1. the taxpayer or a related person held or used the intangible at any time on or after July 25, 1991, and on or before August 10, 1993;
2. the taxpayer acquired the intangible from a person who held it at any time on or after July 25, 1991, and on or before August 10, 1993, and, as part of the transaction, the user of the intangible does not change; or
3. the taxpayer grants the right to use the intangible to a person or a related person who held or used the intangible at any time on or after July 25, 1991, and on or before August 10, 1993.

Who are related persons? A person may be related to another person if engaged in businesses under common control. A 20% ownership test is used to determine the stock and partnership percentages.

An exception to the "anti-churning" rule may apply if the person from whom the intangible is acquired elects to recognize gain on its disposition and pay a tax on the gain which, when added to other income taxes imposed on the gain, equals the product of the gain and the highest rate of income tax applicable to the person. If the election is made, the anti-churning rules apply to the intangible only to the extent that adjusted basis in the intangible exceeds the recognized gain.

The anti-churning rules do not apply to a section 179 intangible acquired from a decedent if the basis of the intangible is stepped up to fair market value.

An amortizable section 197 intangible is not a capital asset. It is treated as depreciable property, and if held for more than one year, it will generally qualify as a section 1231 asset. Amortization claimed on a section 197 intangible is subject to recapture under section 1245 and gain on its sale to certain related persons is subject to ordinary income treatment under section 1239.

Effective dates. Section 197 generally applies to property acquired after August 10, 1993. However, you may elect to apply the provision to all property acquired after July 25, 1991. The election may be revoked only with IRS consent.

LOBBYING EXPENSES DISALLOWED

In the past, certain types of lobbying expenses were deductible business expenses. For example, a business could deduct the cost of lobbying Congress or other legislative bodies concerning legislation that directly affected the business, costs of contacting trade associations about relevant legislation, and also membership dues in a business lobbying group. Grassroots lobbying or political campaign costs were not deductible business expenses. Tax-exempt public charities could generally engage in a limited amount of lobbying; lobbying expenses above the limit were subject to an excise tax. Private foundations were subject to excise tax on all lobbying expenditures. Trade associations and similar organizations were not subject to the excise tax.

New tax law. Under the new law, the following lobbying expenses are not deductible as ordinary and necessary business expenses: (1) influencing legislation; (2) participation in any political campaign for public office; (3) any attempt to influence the general public towards elections, legislation, or referendums; or (4) any direct communication with a covered executive branch official in an attempt to influence official actions or positions.

Lobbying expenses include amounts paid for

research and planning lobbying activities. For example, a taxpayer monitors legislation and later attempts to influence such legislation. The monitoring costs are nondeductible lobbying costs.

Disallowance of charitable deduction. Contributions to organizations which would be otherwise deductible are disallowed if the organization carries on lobbying activities.

Reporting requirement. A tax-exempt organization, other than a charitable organization, claiming business expense deductions must report total nondeductible lobbying expenses for the tax year and dues allocable to such expenses. In addition, the organization must give members a reasonable estimate of the dues allocable to nondeductible lobbying activities. This reporting requirement does not apply to certain in-house expenditures that do not exceed $2,000 for a tax year.

An organization that fails to notify dues payers of nondeductible lobbying expenses may be liable for a tax equal to the product of the highest corporate tax rate for that tax year and the aggregate amount of dues not reported. The special tax is in addition to any interest or penalties that may otherwise apply.

Deductions are allowable for lobbying before certain local councils, such as an Indian tribal council.

6
REAL ESTATE

PASSIVE LOSS BREAK FOR REAL ESTATE PROFESSIONALS

Professional real estate operators have been treated less favorably than other business persons who may deduct losses from businesses in which they materially participate. With the exception of certain rentals and qualifying low-income housing, the ownership of rental property has been treated as a passive activity, regardless of whether or not you participate in operating the property. Thus, rental losses have generally been deductible only against passive income. However, if you manage rental real estate, you may have been able to deduct up to $25,000 of your rental loss; the $25,000 allowance was phased out as adjusted gross income increased from $100,000 to $150,000. The disallowed losses could be carried over to later years, subject to the same restrictions.

The passive law restriction has applied to rentals of apartments and commercial office space (whether long- or short-term); long-term rentals of office equipment, automobiles, and/or a vessel under a bare-boat charter or a plane under a dry lease (no pilot or captain and no fuel); and net-leased property. A property is under a net-lease if the deductions (other than rents and reimbursed amounts) are less than 15% of rental income or where the lessor is guaranteed a specific return or is guaranteed against loss of income.

Rental activities, however, do not include short-term car rentals and rentals of hotel rooms or similar space to transients. Providing incidental services, such as a laundry room in an apartment building, is considered part of the rental activity. Real estate dealers have generally not been treated as engaging in a passive activity. Incidental rentals of investment and business property have generally not been treated as rental activities within the passive activity rules.

If in a nonrental business you also own rental property, you have generally been required to treat the rental activity separately from the nonrental activities. You have not been permitted to group a rental activity with a nonrental activity unless either the rental activity was insubstantial in relation to the business activity, or the business activity was insubstantial in relation to the rental. No guidelines have been provided for determining what is "substantial" for purposes of this test.

Furthermore, you have not been permitted to treat an activity involving the rental of realty and one involving the rental of personal property as a single activity, unless the personal property was provided in connection with the real property.

New tax law. Starting in 1994, the new tax law provides an escape from the rental passive loss restrictions for a broad class of persons who meet activity tests in any real property development, redevelopment, construction, reconstruction, acquisition, conversion, rental, operation, management, leasing, or brokerage trade or business.

Two activity time tests must be met in a taxable year after 1993:

- More than 50% of your personal services in all businesses must be performed in a real property business in which you materially participate.
- More than 750 hours of your services are in real property businesses in which you materially participate.

If you file jointly, the above tests are met if either spouse separately satisfies them.

Personal services performed as an employee are not treated as performed in a real estate business unless you are considered a "5% owner" in the employer. That is, you must own more than 5% of the outstanding stock or more than 5% of total combined voting powers of all stock issued by the corporation. In a noncorporate employer such as a partnership, you must own more than a 5% capital or profit interest.

A closely held C corporation may avoid the rental passive loss restrictions if in a taxable year more than 50% of the gross receipts of the corporation are from real property businesses in which the corporation materially participates.

Generally, each interest in rental property is treated as a separate activity. You may elect to treat all of your interests as one activity.

The ability to meet the material participation tests is greater by aggregating. However, you may not want to aggregate activities if you have passive losses from non-real estate activities and have rental income from an operation which if treated as passive income could be offset by the losses.

The IRS is expected to issue regulations providing its interpretation of the new law and the procedures for making elections.

LONGER DEPRECIATION RECOVERY PERIOD FOR COMMERCIAL BUILDINGS

Under prior law, the recovery period for buildings placed in service after December 31, 1986, was 27.5 years for residential real property and 31.5 years for nonresidential real property. The method of recovery was the straight-line method using a mid-month convention. Under the mid-month convention, all property placed in service or disposed of during any month is treated as placed in service or disposed of at the midpoint of that month. You determine the first-year deduction by applying the percentage from an IRS table.

New tax law. The recovery period for nonresidential buildings is increased from 31.5 years to 39 years. The recovery period of 39 years applies to property placed in service on or after May 13, 1993. The new rate does not apply to property that you place in service before January 1, 1994, if (1) you entered into a binding written contract to purchase or construct the property before May 13, 1993, or (2) you started construction of the property before May 13, 1993.

LOW-INCOME HOUSING CREDIT RENEWED

Prior law. Up until June 30, 1992, a tax credit was allowed in annual installments over ten years for newly constructed or substantially rehabilitated low-income rental housing. For most newly constructed and substantially rehabilitated housing, the credit percentages provided a credit with a present value equal to 70% of the total qualified expenditures. In the case of housing receiving other federal subsidies and the acquisition of an existing building that is substantially rehabilitated, the credit percentages provided a credit with a present value equal to 30% of the total qualified expenditures. Generally, that part of the building for which the credit was claimed had to be rented to qualified low-income tenants at restricted rents for 15 years after the building was placed in service.

To claim a credit the building owner had to receive a credit allocation from a state or local government authority. The allocation from the government agency was provided to the owner on Form 8609. To claim the tax credit on his or her tax return, the owner had to file a copy of the Form 8609 (as well as Schedule A of Form 8609) plus Form 8586, on which the actual credit was computed.

New tax law. The low-income housing credit is made permanent as of June 30, 1992. However, an effective date of August 10, 1993, applies to provisions of the credit relating to (1) tenant occupancy, (2) income recertification, (3) tenant protection, (4) allocations between the buyer and seller, and (5) "HOME" funds. Certain elections must be made within 180 days after August 10, 1993.

TAX RELIEF FOR BUSINESS REALTY DEBT RESTRUCTURING

If your creditor cancels or reduces part of a business realty debt you owe, or the canceled debt secures property you held, you may realize taxable income. For example, a prepayment of a home mortgage at a discount is taxable. However, you are not taxed if you can prove that your creditor intended a gift or you meet certain exemptions allowed by law, such as being bankrupt or insolvent.

New tax law. Under the new law, solvent taxpayers other than C corporations may now elect to avoid tax on a discharge of qualifying real property business debt. Such a discharge may occur where the fair market value of the property securing the debt has fallen in value. A lender may be willing to restructure the mortgage debt by cancelling either all or part of the debt.

The debt must have been incurred to buy, construct, or substantially improve real property used in a business, or to refinance such acquisition debt (up to refinanced amount). The debt must be secured by the property. The new law does not apply to discharges of farm indebtedness, which may be tax free under a separate law.

The tax-free amount may not exceed the excess of the outstanding loan principal (immediately before the discharge) over the fair market value of the real property securing the debt (immediately before the discharge), less any other outstanding debts secured by the property. The excludable amount also may not exceed the taxpayer's adjusted basis for all depreciable real property held before the discharge. The excluded amount reduces the basis of the business real property at the start of the taxable year following the taxable year of the discharge.

Special adjustment rules apply to reduction of debt held by partnerships and S corporations.

The new rule applies to debt discharges after 1992 in taxable years ending after 1992.

Example

On July 1, 1993, Jones, who is solvent, owns a building worth $150,000 used in his business. It is subject to a first mortgage of $110,000 and a second mortgage of $90,000. Jones's basis in the building is $120,000. The second mortgagee agrees to reduce the second mortgage to $30,000. This results in debt discharge of $60,000 ($90,000−$30,000). The $60,000 is considered debt discharge income. But Jones may elect to exclude $50,000. He reports the remaining balance of $10,000 as taxable income. The exclusion limit is calculated as follows:

2nd mortgage before discharge		$90,000
Less: Fair market value of building	$150,000	
Less: Other debt	110,000	40,000
Excludable amount		$50,000

Jones may elect to exclude $50,000 from tax because the basis of the building is sufficient to absorb a basis reduction of $50,000.

7
SECURITIES

OVERVIEW

Capital gain opportunities take on an added luster considering the spread between the new high top income tax rates and the unchanged maximum 28% capital gains rate. An even more favorable but limited capital gain opportunity is created by the capital gain exclusion for certain investments in special small business companies. However, what the government gives, it may take back. The new law restricts capital gain advantages in selected investment areas in which it claims no capital risks are undertaken.

CAPITAL GAIN EXCLUSION FOR INVESTMENTS IN SMALL CORPORATIONS

To encourage investments in certain small businesses, the new law provides a 50% exclusion for capital gains realized on stocks held at least five years in relatively small corporations that meet these tests:

1. The corporation must be a regular C corporation with $50 million or less of aggregate capitalization in debt and equity on or after August 10, 1993. Investments in S corporation stock do *not* qualify for the exclusion.

2. Substantially all of the corporation's assets must be used in the active conduct of a business while the investor is holding the stock. Personal service businesses do not qualify, such as the following businesses: banking, leasing, real estate, farming, mineral extraction and hospitality businesses. An SBICC investment company automatically meets the active business test.

A profitable investment in small business corporation stock qualifies for the exclusion if held at least five years. Stock bought by a partnership or S corporation also qualifies for the exclusion.

The benefit of the exclusion is this: When you sell the stock at a gain after a holding period of at least five years, only 50% of the gain is subject to tax.

Assuming that the maximum capital gains rate remains at 28%, the effective capital gains rate is 14% for an investor in the 28% or over bracket.

Multi-million dollar investments may be subject to this limitation. For each qualifying business, the amount of capital gain for which the exclusion may be claimed is limited to the *greater* of (1) ten times your investment, or (2) ten million dollars (five million if married filing separately).

One half of any exclusion is treated as an AMT preference item.

Ask your broker for available small business corporation investments qualifying for the exclusion.

The exclusion applies to stock issued after August 10, 1993.

TAX DEFERRAL ON SECURITY GAINS INVESTED IN SSBIC STOCK

To encourage investments in small business investment companies (SSBIC), the new tax law gives a tax deferral for gains realized on the sale of publicly-traded securities after August 9, 1993, to the extent the sale proceeds are invested in an SSBIC company. The investment must be made within 60 days of the sale.

The tax deferral is limited annually to the lower of $50,000 or $500,000 reduced by prior tax deferred gains.

The basis of SSBIC stock is reduced by the amount of the nontaxable gain. However, this basis adjustment is not made for purposes of figuring the 50% capital gain exclusion allowed on the sale of SSBIC stock.

EFFECT OF CAPITAL GAINS ON INVESTMENT INTEREST DEDUCTION

Prior law. Net long-term capital gains realized on the disposition of investment property could be treated as investment income for purposes of figuring the "net investment income" ceiling for the investment interest deduction. This was an advantage as it allowed capital gain income to be used as a measure of how much investment interest was deductible.

New tax law. For 1993 and later years, taxpayers who claim the benefit of the 28% maximum rate for net long-term capital gains may not treat such gains as investment income for purposes of figuring how much investment interest is deductible.

This new limitation should apply only where a

taxpayer elects to compute his tax under the 28% tax ceiling because his taxable income is subject to rates exceeding 28%. If this is true, then the new provision should have no effect on the interest deduction claimed by a person in the 15% or 28% bracket. The IRS should release guidelines on this point.

Example

You incur investment interest expenses of $14,000. You have dividend and interest income of $10,000 and long-term capital gain of $5,000. You are in the 31% bracket and elect to use the 28% ceiling to compute tax on long-term capital gains. Under prior law, all of the interest expense was deductible as you had a base of investment income including capital gains exceeding $14,000. Under the new law, you may deduct only $10,000 of investment interest expense because the $5,000 capital gains is not counted in the base. However, if you elect not to take advantage of the 28% tax ceiling, you may treat the capital gains as investment income and deduct the full interest.

RESTRICTIONS AGAINST CAPITAL GAIN CONVERSIONS

What is a "conversion" transaction? It is a transaction generally involving two or more positions taken with regard to the same or similar property, and when reported has the effect of allowing capital gain treatment on what is essentially the earning of interest income. The investor is in the economic position of a lender who expects to receive income while undertaking no significant risks other than those of a lender. The following transactions come within a new law that treats income earned on the transaction as ordinary income.

1. You acquire property and also agree to sell the property or substantially identical property for a determined price.
2. You take offsetting positions on a straddle transaction; or
3. You invest in a transaction marketed or sold as producing capital gain.

Option dealers and commodity dealers are generally exempt from the new limitations.

Ordinary income treatment. In a conversion transaction, the amount of ordinary income from the transaction is not to exceed an "applicable imputed income amount." This is generally the amount of interest that would have accrued on the net investment in the conversion transaction for the period ending on the date of disposition. To figure the interest element, 120% of the applicable federal rate compounded semiannually is used. Lower interest rates may be allowed.

Example

On January 1, 1994, Jones buys stock for $100 and on the same day agrees to sell it to Brown for $115 on January 1, 1996. Assume the applicable federal rate is 5% for purposes of the example. On January 1, 1996, Jones delivers the stock to Brown for $115. Under prior law, Jones would have recognized a capital gain of $15. However, under the conversion transaction rules, $12.36 of the gain is ordinary income ($12.36 is $100 times 6% compounded for two years; 6% is 120% of 5%.) $2.64 is long-term capital gain ($15 − $12.36).

Where a loan finances a conversion transaction and interest is capitalized (under a provision applied to straddles), the amount of ordinary income reported under the new law is reduced.

If the conversion transaction involves a "built-in" loss, the loss is recognized without regard to the new law. For example, if the loss is a capital loss, it remains a capital loss although the conversion rules apply to the transaction.

The new law applies to transactions entered into after April 30, 1993.

MARKET DISCOUNT RULES EXTENDED

All bonds acquired after April 30, 1993, are subject to the market discount rules that treat gain on the disposition of a bond as ordinary income rather than capital gain to the extent of the market discount. Thus, taxable bonds issued before July 19, 1984, and tax-exempt bonds (whatever their issue date), which had been excluded from the market discount rules, are now subject to the rules if acquired after April 30, 1993. An election may be made to report the market discount on an annual basis, instead of at disposition.

OID TREATMENT FOR STRIPPED PREFERRED STOCK

Buyers of stripped preferred stock after April 30, 1993, are now subject to original issue discount (OID) reporting rules. The difference between the stated redemption price and the purchase price is considered OID, a portion of which must be reported as interest income each year.

TAXING UNREALIZED GAINS OF SECURITY DEALERS

Prior law. Security dealers hold substantial inventories of securities. Such inventories allow dealers to sell their clients securities without having to buy them in the market. They are also a source of profit to the dealer if the securities have increased in value over their acquisition cost. However, under prior law, the dealers were allowed to value their year-end inventories at lower of cost or market. This allowed them to escape the reporting of any unrealized gain on securities that have appreciated in value.

New tax law. To tap this source of income for tax purposes, dealers must now value year-end security inventories at market value in taxable years ending after 1993. Adjusted income allocations because of the new rule will be allowed over a 4-year period.

8
TAX PRACTICE

POSSIBLE PENALTY FOR TAKING CONTROVERSIAL POSITIONS

Prior law. Not every transaction has precise tax consequences. Where there is some doubt concerning the tax status of an item, under prior law you could avoid a negligence or substantial understatement penalty for an underpayment of tax attributable to a position taken on a tax return if the position was not frivolous and was adequately disclosed.
New tax law. Starting for returns due after 1993, a "reasonable basis" standard replaces the "not frivolous" standard for purposes of the accuracy-related penalties imposed on taxpayers. The "reasonable basis" standard does not allow you to take a position that is merely arguable. IRS regulations are necessary to flesh out the details of this standard.

The new law does not raise the standard of proof for applying tax penalties against preparers who may still take advantage of the less stringent "not frivolous" standard.

INTEREST-FREE PERIOD GRANTED IRS ON ALL TAX REFUNDS

Prior law. The IRS does not have to pay interest on an income tax refund if the refund is issued within 45 days of the later of the filing due date (without extensions) or the actual filing date. Under prior law, the 45-day rule applied only to original income tax returns. On an amended return showing a refund, the IRS paid interest from the due date of the original return, if timely filed, until a date set by the IRS that was not more than 30 days before the date of the refund check.

New tax law. Starting in 1994, the 45-day interest-free period will apply to all original tax returns—employment, estate and gift tax, excise as well as income tax returns. The IRS does not have to pay interest on original returns if the refund is issued by the 45th day after the later of the due date (without extensions) or the actual filing date.

Amended return filed after 1994. The IRS will not have to pay interest for the period after the filing of the amended return if it pays the refund by the 45th day after the amended return is filed.

9
TAX PLANNING

The increase in tax rates should encourage tax savings plans. Direct your planning sessions to these areas:

- *Investments that return capital gains.* The 28% ceiling on capital gains will provide substantial tax savings opportunities to those subject to top tax rates. Capital gains have been discussed in chapters on "Personal Tax Rate Increases" and "Securities."
- *Investments in tax-exempt bonds that will shelter investment income from tax.*
- *Family income splitting that will shift income taxed in your top bracket to family members in lower tax brackets.* Under prior tax rates, the pressure for income splitting with family members was not as great as was true when rates ranged over the 50% mark. However, the new top rate of 39.6% with the additional effect of the phaseout rules will make family income splitting more attractive. If you can deflect

$1,000 of income taxed at 39.6% to a child's lower bracket of 15%, you would save almost $250. This type of savings is possible with transfers to children who are 14 years or older. Income splitting savings with children under 14 is severely restricted by the "kiddie tax."

- *Deferring income to future years in which you would be in a lower tax bracket.* To prevent a bunching of income in years when the income may be subject to high tax rates, it may be advisable to arrange tax deferral plans. You can defer income through deferred pay plans, qualified retirement plans, transacting installment sales when you sell property, or investing in U.S. Savings Series EE Bonds. However, income deferrals may be illusory and provide little or no savings if your income will not substantially decline during the period when the deferred income would be received. An after-tax dollar in hand for current use or investment may be preferable to an expectation of a tax savings that may not materialize.
- *Reconsidering the use of regular corporate tax reporting.* Under the prior law, personal tax rates generally fell below the regular corporate tax rates. This encouraged business persons to operate through passthrough tax entities, such as partnerships and S corporations. Flowthrough income received by an owner may now be taxable at higher personal rates than income taxable at regular C corporate rates. Therefore,

you should review the effect of your current business tax reporting. This requires careful analysis by an accountant because new elections and corporate tax reporting involve tax consequences other than current tax liabilities. You must realize that regular corporate reporting involves double taxes—(1) the corporate tax and (2) personal taxes on dividend distributions and later dispositions of your stock. Finally, switching between S corporation or partnership reporting and C corporate reporting involves technical adjustments.

INVESTING IN TAX EXEMPTS

Interest on state and local obligations is not subject to federal income tax. It is also exempt from the tax of the state in which the obligations are issued. In comparing the interest return of a tax-exempt with that of a taxable bond, you figure the taxable return that is equivalent to the tax-free yield of the tax-exempt. This amount depends on your tax bracket.

You can compare the value of tax-exempt interest to taxable interest for your tax bracket by using this formula:

Tax-exempt interest return = E
Taxable interest (to be found) = T
Your tax bracket = B

$$T = \frac{E}{1 - B}$$

Example: You are deciding between a tax-exempt bond and a taxable bond. You want to find which will give you more income after taxes. You have a choice between a tax-exempt bond paying 5% and a taxable bond paying 7%. Your projected tax bracket is 36%.

Using this formula, you find that the tax-exempt bond is a better buy in your tax bracket as it is the equivalent of a taxable bond paying 7.8%.

$$T = \frac{0.05}{.64\ (1-0.36)}$$

$$T = .078 \text{ or } 7.8\%$$

The following table shows the amount a taxable bond would have to earn to equal the tax-exempt bond, according to the investor's tax bracket:

If top income tax rate is—	*A tax-exempt yield of— 3%	4%	5%	6%	7%	8%
	is the equivalent of these taxable yields:					
28%	4.2	5.5	6.9	8.3	9.7	11.1
31	4.3	5.8	7.2	8.7	10.1	11.6
36	4.7	6.3	7.8	9.4	10.9	12.5
39.6	5.0	6.6	8.3	9.9	11.6	13.2

*Exemption from the tax of the state issuing the bond will increase the yield.

Ratings of Tax-exempt Bonds. As in the case of commercial bonds, tax-exempt issues are rated by services such as Standard & Poor's and Moody's. In rating a bond, the services will consider the size of the issuer, the amount of its outstanding debt, its past record in paying off prior debts, whether it has competent officials and a balanced budget, its tax assessment and collection record, and whether the community is dominated by a single industry which might be subject to economic change. Generally, an issuer with a good credit rating will offer lower interest rates than one plagued with revenue deficits or similar problems. A basic test is the sufficiency of tax yields or revenues even in times of economic stress.

General obligation bonds will normally be rated higher than revenue bonds because they have the support of the taxing power of the community. Revenue bonds (backed by the revenue of the issuer) may receive high ratings once a capacity to produce earnings is shown.

The interest rate of tax-exempts moves in relation to current taxable market rates. If current market rates drop, the rate of tax-exempts also drops.

In making a specific investment, make a projection of how you believe rates will be in the future. For example, if you expect rates to rise, you might avoid investing in current long-term tax-exempts because an increase in rates would decrease the value of the bonds. Also avoid investing in bonds selling at a premium.

Because investor demand for tax-exempts is high, there are fewer bonds available for investment. Brokers carry various inventories of tax-exempt issues.

Tax-free Money Funds. These funds invest in short-term notes of state and local governments issued in anticipation of tax receipts, bond sales, and other revenue, and in "project notes" issued by local entities and backed by the federal government. The interest paid by these funds is exempt from federal tax. The yields are lower than those of taxable funds, and are attractive only if they provide greater after-tax returns than similar taxable funds. Minimum investments range from $1,000 to $50,000. These funds may offer check writing privileges.

A tax-free interest return may also be available through unit-investment trusts holding tax-exempt state and municipal bonds. These trusts mature in a specified number of years or as called.

RENAISSANCE OF TAX SHELTERS?

With the imposition of higher taxes, promoters may try to take advantage of the taxpayer need for tax shelter plans. Beware! There can be no return to the good old days of tax shelters. The tax law is studded with provisions against tax shelters, including both substantive and penalty provisions. As long as provisions such as the passive loss and interest restrictions stay in place, the prospects of significant tax shelter savings are minimal, except for those areas in which special tax incentives may be offered, such as for low income housing investments. Your test for investments should be based on solid economic expectations that will return capital gains which will be taxed at rates below the top rate.

WILL YOUR STATE TAXES BE AFFECTED BY NEW LAW CHANGES?

Many states base their state income tax on the income which is reported on the federal tax return.

Therefore, any change in your federal adjusted gross income as a result of tax law changes would also show up in your state tax return. For example, a federal change that increases adjusted gross income, such as an increase in the portion of Social Security benefits subject to tax, will generally increase your state income tax. A federal change that decreases your federal adjusted gross income, such as an exclusion for capital gains, will generally decrease your state tax. Keep in mind that even if your state uses federal adjusted gross income as a base, the state may require additions and subtractions to the federal amount, and special state tax rules apply to part-year residents and income from out-of-state sources. Furthermore, state tax rules for personal exemptions, standard deductions and itemized deductions will be different from the federal rules, so your state taxable income will be different from your federal taxable income. Changes in federal itemized deductions, for example, may or may not have an effect on your state return. Here is a list of the states that start with federal income as a base. The District of Columbia also falls in this category.

Arizona
California
Colorado
Connecticut
Delaware
Georgia
Hawaii
Idaho
Illinois
Indiana
Iowa
Kansas
Kentucky
Louisiana
Maine
Maryland
Massachusetts
Michigan
Minnesota
Missouri
Montana
Nebraska
New Mexico
New York
North Carolina
North Dakota
Ohio
Oklahoma
Oregon
Rhode Island
South Carolina
Utah
Vermont
Virginia
West Virginia
Wisconsin

Federal tax deductibility. For taxpayers in some states, a federal tax increase can be fully or partially offset by a deduction for federal tax liability. These states are Alabama, Louisiana, Missouri, Montana, North Dakota, Iowa, Oklahoma, Oregon and Utah.